THE SIGNS OF
THE CHRIST

A New Perspective on the Gospel of John

J. RODNEY TAYLOR

Published by Innovo Publishing, LLC
www.innovopublishing.com
1-888-546-2111

Providing Full-Service Publishing Services for
Christian Authors, Artists & Organizations: Hardbacks, Paperbacks,
eBooks, Audiobooks, Music & Videos

THE SIGNS OF THE CHRIST:
A New Perspective on the Gospel of John

Unless otherwise noted, all Scripture quotations are taken from the
Holman Christian Standard Bible®, Copyright © 1999, 2000, 2002, 2003,
2009 by Holman Bible Publishers. Used by permission. Holman Christian
Standard Bible®, Holman CSB®, and HCSB® are federally registered
trademarks of Holman Bible Publishers.

Library of Congress Control Number: 2017940461
ISBN: 978-1-61314-378-0

Cover Design & Interior Layout: Innovo Publishing, LLC

Printed in the United States of America
U.S. Printing History
First Edition: October 2017

DEDICATION

This book is dedicated to the memory of my beloved Dr. Edward A. McDowell, Jr., Professor of New Testament Interpretation at Southeastern Baptist Theological Seminary. He served as fellow in New Testament Greek under A. T. Robertson from 1928 to 1931, and in 1935 he became a member of the faculty of Southern Baptist Theological Seminary. He joined the faculty at Southeastern in 1952. I had the privilege of serving with him as a graduate assistant. For his intellectual acuity, his encouragement for scholarly pursuit and his Christ-like spirit, I am eternally grateful.

ENDORSEMENTS

"Anytime one travels to an unfamiliar place, it is wise to secure the talents of a guide—someone who knows the terrain and is familiar with the best roads for safe passage. In *The Signs of the Christ: A New Perspective on the Gospel of John*, Dr. Taylor has given us just that. Here we have the insights of an experienced guide whose familiarity with the Gospel writer's territory enables the traveler to navigate to a trove of truth treasure. Any serious Bible student would benefit from this great book!"
—**Mike Harland, Director, LifeWay Worship Resources**

"*The Signs of the Christ* is a journey worth taking, for each 'sign' illustrates the divine authority entrusted to Christ, and each symbol is a further manifestation that He is the person of Christ! Therefore, without reservation, let me recommend for your reading pleasure, *The Signs of the Christ*, by J. Rodney Taylor."
—**Dr. John R. Bisagno, Preacher and Theologian**

"One of the greatest gifts Christians can offer is to write our interpretations of scripture. In this study guide, Dr. Rodney Taylor has provided a treasure to share with others. Dr. Taylor's thoughtful, scholarly reflections on the Gospel of John provide a window into the author's life and a fascinating interpretation of the fourth Gospel. Dr. Taylor brings his lifelong study of scripture, active involvement in church, and deep devotion to Christ to this study. He shows us the value of allowing the Bible to shape a person's life and in turn follow Jesus. Dr. Taylor organizes this study of John around Jesus' signs. He shows us the dramatic way the Fourth Gospel highlights Jesus' divinity and preserves Jesus' humanity. He takes us scene by scene, using careful exposition of scripture while also summarizing John's plot. I recommend using this book while simultaneously reading John or studying this guide with others in a group. Dr. Taylor illuminates the scriptures, adds key insights into the Greek text, and assists the reader to understand John's historical background, themes, and truths. Any student of scripture or Bible study class will grow in their knowledge and faith because of Dr. Taylor's work."
—**William D. Shiell, Ph.D., President & Professor, Pastoral Theology and Preaching, Northern Seminary**

"An author almost never waits until the end of the book to state the purpose for his writing. However, Rodney Taylor reminds the reader that is exactly what the apostle John did in his Gospel. John 20:30-31 reads, "Jesus performed many other signs in the presence of His disciples that are not written in this book. But these are written so that you may believe Jesus is the Messiah, the Son of God, and by believing you may have life in His name.""

Taylor's excellent book reveals the uniqueness of the fourth Gospel. The first three gospels emphasize the human perspective of Jesus, while John's Gospel features His divinity. The Gospel of John is arranged around seven signs and a series of manifestations that characterize Jesus as Messiah rather than a chronology of the life and works of Jesus.

The Signs of the Christ is a useful tool for new believers as they seek to understand that Jesus is fully divine just as he is fully human. It is also a commentary available to pastors, teachers, and theologians who will appreciate the author's careful exegesis of key passages. Taylor demonstrates that each of the signs is 'wrapped in the marvel of a miracle,' revealing the authority of the Messiah and pointing to symbolism beyond itself.

The manifestations of John's Gospel are not proof that Jesus is the Messiah, rather they offer qualities that point to him as a Messianic figure. John writes as an eyewitness of the one who gave his life and was raised from the dead to give life to those who believe. Taylor's book will help us to communicate to believers and nonbelievers alike that Jesus is the Messiah."

—K. Randel Everett, President, 21st Century Wilberforce Initiative

TABLE OF CONTENTS

FOREWORD

Rodney Taylor is an amateur – in the best sense of the word. He does what he does simply for the love of doing it. Rekindling a lifelong love for the gospel of John, Rodney has invited us to a conversation about the Christological signs in John's gospel and how they reveal the person and identity of Christ.

The book is challenging to the lay reader, but not overwhelming. In fact, it would be a great resource for a small group yet, there's enough insight and depth to make a seasoned scholar slow down and think through the deeper insights Rodney brings to us in this book.

Reading *The Signs of the Christ* is like sitting down with a good friend who's as excited about the literature as you are. That's how I felt as I read this book. Rodney loves the gospel of John and is excited to be able to point out all that he's discovered in his studies. Rodney is like the person who visits the museum every day. They can give you the best tour, not because they're paid guides, but simply because they love it so much. As you read, Rodney points out the significance of words, the way John has placed them in his gospel, and best of all, what this discovery tells us about Jesus.

I'm sure, as you read, you'll have the same reaction I had. You'll find yourself loving John's gospel as much as Rodney does. Then, as you close his book, you'll reach for your Bible and open up the gospel of John eager to discover for yourself what Rodney has discovered for us.

Mike Glenn, Senior Pastor
Brentwood Baptist Church

INTRODUCTION

F or a couple of decades I have wanted to write a very special book on the "signs" and "symbols" of the Gospel of John. I must credit my intellectual curiosity for the Gospel of John to my favorite professor in seminary, Dr. Edward A. McDowell. It was one of his choice Gospels, if not his most beloved.

Privileged to serve as his graduate assistant, he often encouraged me to study faithfully the Gospel of John in its original language to ascertain its nuances and to appreciate its distinctiveness. After extensive study of and research upon the Gospel of John, it has truly become my personally favorite Gospel. The appeal of its uniqueness and profundity stimulate intellectual inquiry, and its message begets faith in the Christ it reveals.

It is my sincere hope that this book offers to its readers a new perspective on this wonderful and profoundly theological Gospel. From its pages arise an awareness and insight into Christology found nowhere else in the Bible. John recalls the prophecies, and those prophecies lead him to select carefully the events of Jesus' life that point to a fulfillment of those prophecies. Hence, the Gospel of John is a compendium of Christology unlike any other.

Not intended to be a comprehensive anthology of exegesis and analysis, this particular book is designed to focus on the unique features of the Gospel, primarily its "signs" and symbols." While the book contains an exegesis of selected passages, its principal emphasis is upon the characteristics of the Gospel of John that make it one-of-a-kind, namely its message of Jesus as the Christ through "signs."

This book has been written notably for group study. As a companion to the original textbook itself, I have provided a study guide designed to offer self-study aid and as an interactive protocol to help the Bible student become immersed in the reality of this remarkable Gospel. The study guide: (1) reinforces and clarifies the student's understanding of the textbook material and, (2) develops the student's analytical thinking skills. I have intended that the study guide provide maximum benefit from the student's study time.

I have also offered a teacher's guide designed to assist the facilitator by offering effective teaching/learning procedures that support the learning process. Procedures have been included that will meet the needs of both visual and auditory learners. The guide can be used "as is," or you may feel free to supplement it with ideas of your own. Supplemental resources have been included to strengthen the learning process and offer a bit more factual information. For best results, all three books should be employed as a package.

That being said, this book has also been written for devotional purposes and as a research tool. I have sought to provide a resource that layman, preacher and researcher alike can understand and apply its message. The text contains an analysis of key Greek terms, but they are identified both in the Greek and by Arabic lettering, and their meanings are identified in detail. The analysis of the "signs" and "symbols" are based upon years of research and study and reflect my best judgment on their purpose and meaning. May the effort here be beneficial to the reader's knowledge of and faith in Jesus as the Christ. To that end, this book has been written.

Chapter One
Introduction – John 1:18

Introduction

John is the most distinctive of the four Gospels because of its unique perspective. He paints a portrait of Jesus designed to illustrate conclusively that this Bethlehem-born Jew, raised in a modest home by working-class parents was, indeed, the long-expected Messiah. His perspective is described in vv. 30-31 in chapter 20. More concisely the view of this grand Gospel can be summed up in a single word—Christology. What this means is that John's whole purpose was to set about to proclaim who Jesus is Messianicly. And in order to do this, he set forth the meaning of Jesus in ways and in power unparalleled in the other Gospels. Some of the ways that John's Gospel is distinct from the Synoptics include:

What it omits. There is no mention of:

1. The temptation
2. The transfiguration

3. Words of institution of the Lord's Supper

4. The Ascension event

5. Choosing of the Twelve

6. The Sermon on the Mount

7. Jesus' birth story

8. Baptism of Jesus

9. No mission of the Twelve or the Seventy

10. No Lord's Prayer

11. No Gethsemane

12. Minor roles attributed to the great parables of Jesus

Distinctive in what the Gospel adds:

1. Miracle at Cana

2. Incident with Nicodemus

3. Encounter with the woman at the well

4. Healing of the lame man at the pool of Bethesda

5. Healing of the man born blind

6. Teaching of the Good Shepherd

7. Raising of Lazarus

8. Washing the Apostles' feet

9. The Intercessory Prayer of Jesus (High Priestly Prayer in chapter 15)

10. The farewell discourses of chapters 13-17

11. Greeks who came to Jesus

Other differences:

1. Jesus spent more time in Judea than iⁱ ‗‗‗‗‗ (reversed in the Synoptics).

2. The Cleansing of the Temple occurs at the beginning of Jesus's ministry in John, chapter 2. Both Mark (11:15-18) and Luke (19:45-48) place this cleansing at the close of Jesus' ministry immediately following His triumphal entry into Jerusalem.

3. The Last Supper appears to be held on the eve of Passover as opposed to two days before as in the Gospel of Mark.

4. Jesus is proclaimed openly as the Messiah at the beginning of His ministry. In Mark, for example, it does not occur until chapter 8 with Peter's confession.

A thorough review of the Gospel reveals the absence of several of the great themes that appear in the Synoptics. At least three of these themes include:

1. ἡ βασιλεία τοῦ θεοῦ (hē basileia tou theou), "the kingdom of God," only occurs once in this Gospel.

2. ὁ ἔσχατος (ho eschatos), the concept of eschatology, is missing from the text of John.

3. τὸ εὐαγγέλιον (to euangelion), the "good news," will not be found in this Gospel.

The major question is "why"? Why are these characteristics unique to or absent from the Gospel of John? The most plausible answer to that question is that John wished to provide a different portrait of Jesus, a more spiritual interpretation of His life. Whereas the

Synoptics took a more human view of Jesus, John wished to emphasize His divinity. In order to achieve this mission, he tended to heighten the supernatural aspects of Jesus, such as His omniscience and His power.

John preserves a valuable body of traditional sayings, parables, and dialogues which were drawn from the same general reservoir as those of the Synoptic Gospels. So it is likely that John is using authentic material found elsewhere and has drawn out its spiritual and Messianic meaning for the Christian faith. This approach is what gives the Gospel its distinctive value. John is not interested in setting forth a chronology of the life of Jesus. He chooses his material and places it where he does in order to set forth plainly who Jesus is and the difference he makes. John is not governed by chronology but by meaning.

Purpose

The author states his specific reason for writing this Gospel in 20:30-31, "These are written," he says, "so that you may believe Jesus is the Messiah, the Son of God." One cannot fully understand the perspective of John without a complete grasp of these verses. He implements this purpose within a Hebrew framework, i. e., by employing the Greek χριστὸς (*christos*) which is derived from χρίω (*chriō*), to anoint. This term occurs thirteen times in the Gospel, more than any of the individual Synoptics. From the beginning, John did not intend to write a biography or a chronological accounting of Christ; he selected certain events of Jesus's ministry that would identify Jesus as the Christ. Then he arranged them into episodes in such a way that the final result is a drama, in epic proportion, of the Word becoming flesh (1:14).

In a genuine sense, the Gospel of John is a classic study in Christology from beginning to end. It is a convincing argument, based on personal experience, in favor of the Messiahship of Jesus. Dr. A. T. Robertson wrote, "John gives us his deliberative, mature, tested view of Jesus Christ as shown to him while alive and as proven since his resurrection."[1] Alfred Plummer wrote, ""It was not John's purpose to write a complete 'Life of Christ;' it was not his purpose to write a 'Life' at all. Rather he would narrate just those facts respecting Jesus which would produce a saving faith as the Messiah and Son of God."[2] Since the author is concerned to set forth the meaning of Jesus to eyes of faith, he does not find it necessary to include as many details or as many episodes as do the Synoptics. John is interested not so much in the God who sent Jesus as he is in the Jesus whom God sent. The tenor of his objective permeates the words of 20:30-31.

Authorship

A consensus of scholars attributes this gospel to John, the Beloved disciple. Evidence from the church Fathers of such authorship is quite convincing. Irenaeus, the bishop of Lyons, in his *Against Heresies*, affirms that John wrote this Gospel while in Ephesus in Asia. Irenaeus had heard the stories from Polycarp, a contemporary of John who had heard these accounts personally from John. Tertullian, in *Against Marcion*, wrote that John was the author, and Clement of Alexandria basically took the Johannine

---

1. A. T. Robertson, *The Divinity of Christ in the Gospel of John*, New York: Fleming H. Revell Company, 1916.
2. A. Plummer, *The Gospel According to John*, Cambridge: University Press, 1891, 366.

authorship for granted. Eusebius wrote in his *History of the Church* that "John wrote a spiritual gospel."[3]

A renowned professor of mine, with whom I both studied and for whom I taught Greek and New Testament as a graduate assistant, Dr. Edward A. McDowell, based his conclusion on the authorship of the Gospel upon the tradition of these church Fathers. He held that John, the son of Zebedee, also known as the Beloved disciple, and the "disciple whom Jesus loved," may perhaps not have personally authored the Gospel. Rather he may have shared with a younger man his reminiscences of Jesus and collaborated on the Gospel, especially as to what would be its purpose and format.

In three passages of the Gospel, the author testifies to the fact that he was a witness to the life about which he writes. In 1:14 he asserts the authority of an eyewitness; 19:35 supports that declaration just as strongly; and at 21:24 he declares that his words are first-hand, not hearsay.

The author of this Gospel was likely a Palestinian Jew by birth and was familiar with the Law and the observances of the faith. Plummer writes, "The form of the gospel, especially the style of the narrative, is essentially Jewish. The language is Greek, but the arrangement of the thoughts, the structure of the sentences, and a great deal of the vocabulary are Hebrew."[4] The writer's familiarity with the geography of the region also supports an authorship by a Palestinian Jew. Examples of his awareness of the territory can be found in 1:28, 11:18, 11:54, and 21:2.

The author, or his collaborator, was at least an eyewitness of the events about which he wrote historically. He was well acquainted with Palestine, and so it is not difficult to assume that John the Apostle, who was both

---

3. Eusebius, *History of the Church* 6:25.
4. Plummer, *op. cit.*, 25.

a disciple of Jesus and a Palestinian Jew, was most likely the author or co-author (collaborator) of the Gospel which bears his name.

Date

Modern archeological finds, such as the John Rylands Fragment, provide evidence of a fairly early date. The Rylands Fragment 457 contains a small portion of the Gospel of John in Greek and has been dated about 135 AD meaning that the Gospel was actually in circulation in codex or book form in Egypt as early as 125 AD. With the early development of the Jewish ideas found in these archeological fragments likely having taken place during the first century and their inclusion in the Gospel of John supports an early date.

Another scholarly position on the date is that the Gospel was written late in the life of John, perhaps 85-90 AD. Such a theory is based upon the belief that the author gives a "reflective account" of the ministry of Jesus and seems to look back on those experiences with Jesus after a long lapse of time. The Gospeler creates a kind of picture album of the life of Christ as an expression of His Messiahship demonstrated through "signs."

The Dead Sea Scrolls also contribute to the dating of the Gospel. They contain descriptions of a type of Hellenistic Judaism that existed in the early first century. These writings provide evidence of the development of Greek thought in Judaism sufficiently early to have allowed the writer of the Gospel to be familiar with it. The date of authorship likely occurred in the decade of 70-80 AD, written with the aid of a collaborator from Ephesus, the home of the Apostle John.

Occasion

The elders and disciples of the churches in Asia may have requested that John write the account of Jesus and his ministry which he had preached many times. After the destruction of Jerusalem, Christianity needed a new interpretation of the message of Christ. Pagan-Christian philosophy, namely Gnosticism, was quickly infiltrating the early church. This heresy demanded a clear, authoritative statement of Christianity which presented Jesus as the Christ, the Son of God.

While it is my supposition that John was familiar with the writings of the Synoptics, nevertheless, he produced an independent account of the life of Christ. An example can be found in the comparison of John 1:19f with Mark 19:17f that reveals two contradictory versions of the identification of Elijah. A reading of John 6:5f indicates that Jesus precipitated the feeding of the five thousand, a fact which Matthew and Mark corroborate but Luke describes as having been initiated by the disciples. No detailed account of the Last Supper appears in the Gospel of John (13:1f). While he mentions that a "supper" occurred, John's version is short on details simply because he wishes rather to emphasize the washing of the disciples' feet. In John, this event occurs just before Passover, and if the Synoptics are correct, then John actually moved the crucifixion up by 24 hours. Numerous other examples could be given, but these are sufficient to support the independent nature of the writing.

There appears also to have been an Ephesian tradition associated with this Gospel. By a reading of the Epistle to the Ephesians there seems to exist a body of teaching provided to the Ephesian church by an eyewitness. Some scholars postulate that the eyewitness might have been

John the Beloved, natural to conclude since John was a native of Ephesus and had preached there often.

Two well-defined strands of tradition developed at Ephesus. One was the distinct teachings of Paul, especially those respecting the wisdom of God and the spirit. The second tradition was Paul's interpretation of Christ. Paul considered Christ to be the ὁ υἱὸς τοῦ θεοῦ (*ho huios tou theou*), the "son of God," the one who is pre-existent with God. The Fourth Gospel acknowledges these two strands of tradition and interprets Jesus Christ on the basis of them. The author, as an interpreter, expressed his authority by using the sources available to fit his individual purpose.

What may we then conclude so that a proper direction and acceptable interpretation may be reached? First, it is critical that one accept the emphasis upon the human Jesus. He was the "divine-man," as much human as he was divine, as much divine as he was human. Second, accept the validity of the claims that the Gospel is the testimony of an eyewitness. By acceding to this claim, speculation and digression are avoided.

Third, recognize and acknowledge that the writer of this Gospel was a poet, a dramatist and a theologian. By doing so, the heightening of the supernatural colors in Jesus is allowed. Although John acknowledged the historical Jesus, he was more focused on the heavenly Christ of Paul than with the man Jesus.

Fourth, accept the irrelevancy of the historical and non-historical properties of the events. John did not involve history for the sake of history or to prove a point. His was an interpretation of history and the facts of a particular event only provided him with a framework within which to tender his interpretation.

Relation to the Epistles

Which was written first, the Gospel or the Epistles? Any conclusion is speculation, however, because the content of this Gospel was transmitted through an oral tradition before it was written, it is possible that the Epistles were actually penned before the physical writing of this Gospel. It is likely safe to conclude that both the Gospel and the Epistles were written within just a few years of each other.

While a study of both the Gospel and the Epistles reveals minor similarities and differences, the major difference is their perspectives. The purpose of the Gospel was to "create a conviction"[5] that the human Jesus was the long-awaited Messiah. The Epistles, rather, declare that the Messiah is Jesus. Plummer describes the difference by writing, "The Gospel starts from the historical human teacher and proves that he is divine; the Epistles start from the Son of God and contend that he has come in the flesh."[6] Since the Epistles were probably written by the same person, alike yet different is one's best conclusion.

Prologue 1:1-18

John begins his Gospel with a brief passage which marks it off from the other gospels. This prologue is the foundation upon which the remainder of the Gospel is written. In fact, the story of Jesus, which formally begins in 1:19, is based upon the understanding of Jesus that is contained in the prologue. It sets forth major theological emphases which unfold in the interpretation of Jesus. This interpretation continues from verse 19 to the end of the book.

---

5. Plummer, *op. cit.*, 51.
6. *Ibid.*

The great affirmation of the prologue is that ὁ λόγος τοῦ θεοῦ (*ho logos tou theou*), the "Word of God," that is, God's personal, creative and redeeming activity entered history to live a genuine historical life in the man Jesus. The prologue is written solely to introduce the *logos*. For the first five verses John deals with the *logos* in eternity. In verses 6-18 he describes the *logos* in history.

The term "*logos*" (logos), translated "word," calls for special attention. It has been found among the Stoics as "rational principle" in the *Hermetica*[7], as divine power and the medium of salvation in Hellenistic religions and in Philo as the divine instrument by which the knowledge of God is revealed.

To Philo the *logos* was not a personality, but it was not impersonal either. In fact, Philo's idea, which may have been derived from Plato, considered the *logos* to be the image of God from which man was created. However, Philo's *logos* falls short of that of John because Philo never considered the *logos* to be a person. Philo's idea of God precluded the possibility that he could become flesh.

Judaism, by John's time, had come to the conclusion that *logos* referred to God's self-expression in word and deed. The Jews understood Word or *logos* in terms of Wisdom and Law. John's sense of *logos* went beyond any contemporary ideas because he looked upon the Word as God's personal and creative activity manifested supremely when the Word became flesh.

Therefore, whether the reader of the Gospel were a Gentile familiar with the philosophies of the Greco-Roman world or a Jew conversant with wisdom, the Law and the Prophets, that reader would have been attracted by this term. You see, a Greek considered the *logos* as some

---

7. *Hermetica* or *Corpus Hermeticum* are ancient Egyptian writings produced during the height of Greek and Latin philosophy.

impersonal, rational reality. A Jew considered the *logos* as God's self-expression. John considered the *logos* as God's personal creative activity, incarnate in a human life (1:14). Because of John's use of this term, it is likely that he meant to present the claims of Jesus as fulfillment of both Jewish and Gentile hopes. And the use of this term would attract both.

John's employment of the term is religious, not philosophical. He speaks only of the Word in reference to creation. Paul used it in reference to redemption in Colossians 1:13-20 and the writer of Hebrews used it in that same context in 1:1-4. But John focused on its theological significance.

In verse one of the Prologue, John offers three qualities of the *logos*.

1. His eternity ("In the beginning")
2. His fellowship with God ("the Word was with God")
3. His divine nature ("the Word was God")

Verses 6-13 describe the work of the "Announcer," the "Forerunner." Not one to draw attention to himself, John's responsibility was to announce the arrival of the Messiah. Portraying the Messiah as "the Light," the Announcer proclaimed first that he was not the Light, only the one bearing witness to the Light, thus avoiding the adulation of the multitudes.

In verse 11 John explained the tragic nature of Jesus' coming. His advent was acknowledged neither by humankind in general nor by His own people, the Jews. The words translated "own" are written in two different forms, the first a feminine, the second a masculine form. The first "own" connotes that the true Light came to his "own" humankind; the second "own" refers to His "own" people, the Jews, who rejected Him. John emphasizes this fact here even as Paul struggled with the same rejection in Romans 9-11. Nevertheless, those who did receive and acknowledge Him, to them, by grace, He offered kinship as sons of God.

Verse 14 is John's record of the Christmas story summed up in the most poignant yet profound declaration to be found in the entire Scriptures. The word translated here as "dwelt" is the Greek ἐσκήνωσεν (*eskēnōsen*) meaning "pitch a tent" or "tabernacle." It is a reference to the *shekinah* of the Old Testament where God "dwelt" among his people in the form of a pillar of cloud by day and a pillar of fire by night. It can also mean "presence" and refer to the dwelling presence of God in Jesus. The profundity of its meaning is often lost, but it really denotes that God the Father saw fit to send Himself in fleshly form to experience life even as you and I experience life. John is stating in simple terms that the "*logos* was an act of Divine love."[8] But most important of all, it is the incarnation of Christ that becomes the meeting place of God and man.

John's perspective of the *logos* was as an eyewitness. So not only did he identify Jesus as the *logos*, but he also witnessed Him as the glory of the Father. He employs δοξα (*doxa*), "glory," to point to the source of his Divine nature. He is the "glory of God." While the "glory of God" can possess multiple meanings in the New Testament, John utilizes the term to refer to the self-revelation of God. He acknowledged that he had witnessed the "glory of God" in both the human form and the ministry of Jesus. The "glory" about which he writes is a confession of faith in God's fundamental being and revealed character.

---

8. R. H. Strachan, *The Fourth Gospel*, London: SCM Press, Ltd., 1941, p. 102.

Because he has witnessed the revealed "glory of God," he can write with certainty that Jesus is the long-sought Messiah and the fulfillment of Jewish law. He acknowledges that fulfillment in verse 17.

What, then, can we conclude about the prologue?

1. It is a striking effort to attract the attention of both Jewish and Greek readers.

2. The author's use of the prologue is religious, not philosophical.

3. The prologue sets forth the major theological emphases or themes which unfold in the interpretation of Jesus beginning in 1:19.

4. The prologue constitutes John's distinctive way of introducing his understanding of Jesus in reference to the other gospels.

5. The prologue is a confession of faith set to music. It is either a hymn or a passage of lyrical prose.

The wisdom of John's assertion in these first eighteen verses lies firmly and profoundly in the Incarnation. Hoskyns wrote: "Jesus has taken the place of the Temple, and His Sonship is . . . greater than the Temple. Jesus gives men more than the Temple or the Jewish people ever had given, and His disciples take the place of the Jews. In the perspective of the gospel the abiding of the Word of God in flesh merges in the abiding of the Son of God in all those who believe in Him."[9] So now the dwelling of Jesus on this earth abides in us who believe that He is the Son of God and whose Spirit dwells within us eternally.

---

9. Edwin Clement Hoskyns, *The Fourth Gospel*, London: Faber and Faber Limited, 1947, 148.

Chapter Two
John 1:19 – 2:22

The Witness, 1:19-28

J ohn takes this opportunity to introduce Jesus to the nation of Israel and to enlighten the disciples regarding who Jesus is. Three elements comprise this introduction:

1. John illustrates **how** the Word (*logos*) was made flesh in the world as a real man, vv. 19-30. Quick to set the priests and Levites straight, John deflects their insistence that he declare himself to be the Christ or Elijah or the Prophet. He clarifies his baptism and subordinates himself and his baptism to the work and ministry of Jesus the man.

2. John demonstrates how the Word made flesh is, in fact, the Messiah of Israel, vv. 31-34. He wants, more than anything, for his followers to understand that this man about whom he speaks has been validated by God Himself in the sign of the dove. He is, indeed, the Messiah, and John will present the "signs" that God has offered through His ministry

to authenticate that He is the Messiah of Israel.

3. John explains how the experience of men and their perception of Messiahship is based upon what they see, vv. 35ff.

Referring to the "witness" of v. 7, John now expands upon that witness. While in Bethany following Jesus' baptism, John is confronted by an inquisitive group of priests and Levites from the Sanhedrin. Being the Supreme Court of Judaism, the members of the Sanhedrin issued judgments which served as the final authority on any religious dispute or problem. Its power was felt throughout the Jewish world of that time, and to be confronted by members of the Sanhedrin would sometimes strike fear in the hearts and minds of those confronted.

These priests and Levites are troubled by John's popularity and inquire as to his reason for stirring up trouble through unsanctioned religious services. After all, he was engaged in baptizing, a uniquely religious rite. The Jewish Levitical laws specified the procedure for ritual washings for physical human conditions that were considered to be unclean. These ritual washings morphed into the practice of baptism by immersion as seen in Hebrews 9:10. The Jews did not perceive that these ritual washings simply involved scrubbing or rubbing to remove contamination. They believed that immersion, the *mikveh*, required the complete submersion of the body in water and that the water should contact every part of the body. Baptism by immersion was also required of all who converted to Judaism.

The priests and Levites who approached John were likely familiar with his priestly heritage (see Luke 1)—he was not unknown to them—so they assumed that he was intentionally engaging in a priestly function. They confront him and asked, "Under what authority do you think you can conduct this religious rite, when we have not given you the license to do so?"

John is troubled by their attitudes. Moreover, he is perplexed by their misconstruction of his message, and so, to put their minds at ease, he strongly denies being the Messiah. "I am **not** the Messiah." In fact John is not anyone they presuppose him to be.

His response, however, did not satisfy their thirst for truth. They were astounded because he spoke as one with authority, yet he was not "one of them." The Jews had long associated both Moses and Elijah with the coming of the Messiah, so their inquiries were sincere, though misguided. What they sought from John was credibility and credentials, but he only offered the simplicity of repentance coupled with humility.

The declaration that he is the Forerunner of Christ is unmistakable. John the Gospeler writes in retrospect from the perspective of history, having witnessed and recollected the crucifixion of his Lord by the Jews. His calling as a Forerunner inspired him to preach a new kind of baptism, a baptism of repentance.

Openly he affirms (v. 26) that the Christ is, indeed, among them, but they do not recognize Him. John's purpose in this affirmation is to "announce" that Old Testament prophecy has now been fulfilled, and he is only a voice that calls for faith in that fulfillment. Robertson rephrases John's objective: "I am not a prophet to foretell His coming, but a herald to proclaim that He has come."[10] Then Robertson paraphrases an early rabbinical saying from around 250 BC, "Every service which a servant will perform for his master, a disciple will do for his Rabbi, except loosing his sandal

---

10. Robertson, *op. cit.,* 74.

thong."[11] By adding this Jewish proverb, John is declaring that One has come who is such a Rabbi's Rabbi that I, like any loyal disciple, am not worthy to loose His sandals. By sharing this quotation, John emphasized that his mission to preach repentance was far less important than the mission and ministry of Jesus.

Worthy is the Lamb, 1:29-34

Verse 29 comprises the crescendo of this chapter. Publicly John declares that Jesus is the Messiah and identifies Him with the Suffering Servant of Isaiah (53). This concept was not unknown among the Jews, however, John blends the efficacy of the Passover lamb and its accompanying symbolism of a unique relationship with Jehovah with the imagery of the Suffering Servant. After all, John's objective is to "emphasize the heavenly rather than the Galilean origin of Jesus."[12] Such blending accentuates the role of Christ "inasmuch as Jesus as the 'Lamb of God' cannot 'take away' sin without taking it on Himself."[13]

Even John admits that he did not initially recognize Jesus as the Messiah. It was revealed to him (3:27). John's call from God was to preach a gospel of repentance which included baptism, a baptism of repentance, and to make Christ known to Israel. Then unexpectedly he was approached by Jesus to be baptized. Consider now the unique circumstances in which John finds himself.

He is preaching repentance and baptizing those who accept his message when suddenly appears this One upon

---

11. Hermann L. Strack and Paul Billerbeck, *Kommentar Neuen Testament aus Talmud und Midrash*, Munich: C. H. Beck'sche Verlagsbuchhandlung, 1922, I, 121.

12. Hoskyns, *op. cit.*, 175.

13. Strachan, *op. cit.*, 115.

whom John observed the Spirit of God in the form of a dove. John inwardly acknowledged that Jesus did not require a baptism of repentance, and he balked at the prospect.

How did John recognize the Spirit in the form of a dove? The acceptance of the Spirit-dove probably can be traced to the story of the Flood when Noah sent out two birds, one of which was a dove, a symbol of gentleness. Returning with an olive branch, a traditional symbol of peace, the Spirit descended as a dove to rest upon the Prince of Peace.

So acting upon God's symbolic message, John baptized Jesus. It is that witnessed event to which John refers so directly and unequivocally in vv. 32-34.

The First Disciples, 1:35-51

Jesus began His ministry by calling His first disciples. In addition to John the Beloved Disciple (referred herein as the Gospeler), the two men described in v. 35, both of whom were likely disciples of John the Baptist, had probably heard about Jesus from John. Upon seeing Him and hearing John's declaration that He was the "Lamb of God," they followed without hesitation. Andrew is identified as one of the two disciples, and tradition presumes that John the brother of James might have been the other.

Andrew finds his brother, Simon, and tells him that he has found the Messiah. What a confession! Upon meeting Simon face to face, Jesus recognizes and acknowledges his steadfast character, his stony countenance, and so re-identifies him as "Cephas." This name, meaning "rock" in Aramaic, is translated into the Greek as *petros* (*petros*), Peter.

The next day Jesus found Himself again in the area where Andrew and Peter lived. He found Philip, who located Nathaniel and told him that the Messiah had come. Upon calling them, both joined the ranks of the disciples.

Consider the diversity of character and experience of these first disciples. First, John, the Beloved disciple, is the spiritual leader. Then Andrew (identified as Bartholomew in the Synoptic Gospels) seems to have been the "go to" guy as illustrated in 6:8 and 12:22. Whenever and wherever there was a need or an issue he was consulted.

Simon, now known as Peter, is characterized by a strong will, sometimes obstinate, but a skillful leader. As a result Peter often served as the spokesperson for the band of disciples. A fisherman by trade, he had mastered the art of disappointment, when, after a long night on the sea, his nets contained little to show for his efforts. He wanted to give up, give in to his tired physical condition. But he was also a man of determination, and it may have been that characteristic that attracted Jesus to include him in the group.

Philip may be equated to a modern accountant, skilled at practicality. At the feeding of the five thousand, it was Philip who calculated the estimated cost of the event (6:7). Such a pragmatic thinker would bring a special, level-headed character to this group.

Finally, Nathaniel joined with Jesus as a disciple. Jesus acknowledged the faithfulness of Nathaniel to his Jewish heritage. In Nathaniel, Jesus found no "guile," no duplicity, no treachery (1:47). He was a Jew's Jew and "represented Rabbinic Judaism at its best."[14] He had grown up in Cana not far from Nazareth. These two cities were often rivals, and it was Nathaniel's knowledge of this competitiveness that prompted his comment "Can anything good come out of Nazareth?" (1:46)

For the first time in v. 51, Jesus refers to Himself as the "Son of Man." This title, derived by the Israelites from

14. Strachan, *op. cit.,* 120.

Daniel 7:13-14, came to be identified with the long-sought Messiah. However, Jesus' use of the term here to refer to Himself as the Messiah is doubted by some scholars.[15] Whether Jesus' quoting of the phrase is intentional or not, John surely employed the term as a means of offering a preamble to the first of his Christological signs.

The Signs

Have you ever read the ending chapter of a book before picking up the story at the beginning? John peculiarly wrote the purpose of his treatise at the end, and the reader is not privy to his reasoning until that point. So let's begin at the end.

John 20:30-31 reads: "Jesus performed many other signs in the presence of His disciples that are not written in this book. But these are written so that you may believe Jesus is the Messiah, the Son of God, and by believing you may have life in His name."

What are "signs"? In the Synoptic Gospels the Greek word for sign, σημεῖον (sēmeion) can be translated as a sign, indication or mark and usually referred to the end time (Luke 21:25; Matthew 24:30); occasionally it defined a miracle to prove a point. Tenney adds that it might also refer to an impending catastrophe.[16] In John, however, "sign" refers to seven specific events—all miracles—which John has identified to be indicators or "proofs" that occur in present, earthly time but that testify to and affirm Jesus' Messiahship. That is the key, Messiahship. The word "sign" is consistently and uniquely associated by John with the word "Messiah."

---

15. One of those scholars is Alfred Plummer.

16. Merrill C. Tenney, "Topics from the Gospel of John, Part II: The Meaning of the Signs," *Bibliotheca Sacra* 132 (April 1975), 145.

John includes seven "signs" in his Gospel. Recall in Hebrew thought that the number seven represented completeness, fulfillment or spiritual perfection. Numerous examples of its use can be found throughout the Bible. For example, God created the world in seven days; the Book of the Revelation includes seven trumpets, seven seals and the seven bowls of wrath; Jesus is reported to have spoken seven final words on the cross. John, then, employs seven "signs" to direct attention to the confirmation of Jesus as the Messiah, to reveal the completeness of God's revelation to mankind. John was careful to fulfill his purpose by ensuring that each "sign" was also a declaration, an announcement, an assertion that Jesus was the Christ.

In order for John to qualify an event as a "sign," it must pass the litmus test of four criteria. First, the "signs" all were wrapped in the marvel of a miracle. Each was of supernatural origin and sourced from the Father. Jesus alone is the unique source of the miracle performed, and through the miracle, He portrays a deeply spiritual message. These miracles were not simply magic tricks or hypnotic allusions, but they were of supernatural character, of no ordinary human origin, simply the real results of the work of God through Jesus. These miracles were not transitory or temporary in nature but permanent.

Second, the miracle must include the participation of others in the miracle either directly or indirectly. The participatory element of each "sign" played a key role in its authentication. Participation may mean simply expressing belief in Jesus' ability to heal as in the case of the nobleman's son, or it may mean actually performing a ritual as in the case of the healing of the blind man. Although Jesus never needed the help of anyone, He chose to allow others to enjoy and appreciate the benefit of sharing in the miracle.

Third, the miracle must have been witnessed by others than Jesus and the one experiencing the miracle. In this way a spiritual message is proclaimed, and there are witnesses who can corroborate the miracle and testify to its authenticity.

Finally, the miracle possesses a unique symbolism; it must point beyond itself. It features an Old Covenant-New Covenant component in which an element of the narrative, either a person or feature, will point to the Old Covenant, Israel. Another element points to the New Covenant, the church or the New Israel. By employing such symbolism, witnesses may not have been immediately aware of the significance of the event with respect to Jesus' Messiahship, but subsequent events and the final "sign" testify loudly to the fact that He was, indeed, the Son of God; He **was** the Messiah.

Each "sign" pointed to the fulfillment of prophecy or revealed the beginning of the New Order in Christ as contrasted with the Old Order under Jewish Law. In each case the "sign" points backward to the Old Testament and forward to the ultimate "sign," the death and resurrection of Jesus.

Each of the "signs" illustrated some aspect of His divine authority. Jesus always affirmed that He did nothing apart from the Father, so each "sign" possessed the imprimatur of the Father, because it "shouted" to the world that Jesus was and remains the Christ of history.

Introductory Sign, 2:1-12

Before describing the public manifestations of Jesus as the Messiah, John introduces a preliminary "sign," replete with symbolism but effectual to any Jew. During the time that John associated with Jesus, he purposely selected individual miracles and included them in this specific order for a purpose—that is, to open the eyes of the unbeliever to faith in the real Christ and gain eternal life. The pre-existent Holy Spirit, through the Gospel writer, uses these miracle stories to present the true Christ to an unbelieving heart.

In the Synoptics miracles demonstrate the Kingdom of God as described in the casting out of the demons in Matthew 12:28, but in the Gospel of John they point unambiguously to the nature of Jesus. Note in 12:36[17] that only men of faith recognize and acknowledge these "signs," because they testify to the power and glory of God in Jesus. They are "proofs" of the arrival of the long-awaited Messianic age.

The wedding at Cana of Galilee (approximately nine miles north of the city of Nazareth) is recorded nowhere else in the New Testament. It is manifestly appropriate to be written as an introductory "sign," employed by John to reveal the infinite glory of God in Jesus, to reveal what He was and the kind of Messiah He would be.

The wedding occurred on the seventh day following His baptism. By choosing the seventh day for this "sign," John acknowledged that Jesus was the fulfillment of the One whom the Jews had anticipated for millennia. His life and death were to be the culmination of God's plan from the foundation of the world. John affirms in one number, seven, that He came to complete a mission assigned by the Father to bring salvation to lost humanity.

To introduce his aim in writing this Gospel, John selects a story from the non-traditional records of Jesus' ministry and initiates the achievement of his purpose by using this common event to paint a picture of the fulfillment of Jewish prophecy in the man, Jesus. The wedding party, many of

---

17. "While you have the light, believe in the light so that you may become sons of light." John 12:36

whom may have been friends of Jesus' family, was in the third day of a seven-day celebration. During such a lengthy celebration, it was necessary for the host of the feast to prepare sufficient food and wine to provide for the guests. So when the wine was exhausted, Mary instinctively asked her son to assist, confident that He could furnish whatever was lacking for the proper conclusion of the feast.

His response, typical for the Gospel of John, is simply "woman," γυνή (gunē). Nowhere within this Gospel does Jesus ever refer to his mother by name. While it sounds a bit cold, gunē actually is not. This expression is the same word that Jesus used on the cross when He said, "Woman, here is your son," and committed her to John. Put into today's vernacular, it would best be translated as "lady." Rather than a term of disrespect, it is a warm compliment.

So why does Jesus not call her mother? Had Jesus called her "mother," He would have been emphasizing His human relationship to her. The time for her authority as His earthly mother is complete; she must now lose her son to a high purpose, to a higher mission--to the world. After all, this is the destiny that was laid upon her. When He called her "lady," in effect He was saying, "I'm God. It is no longer a human relationship. You are now conversing with the Son of God."

For the first time here, Jesus obscurely suggests His ultimate purpose. "My hour has not yet come" is a heavenly response to a practical, earthly suggestion. She had asked for a simple favor, He purposed the occasion for a divine revelation, but the time was not right. The term "hour," ὥρα (hōra), occurring seven times in this Gospel, refers to the hour of His glorification, when He will, by His blood, bring to completion His mission on earth, cleanse from sin those who believe in Him and bestow eternal life upon them. Until that special "hour," the actions of Jesus are merely signs of what He is. How was she to know that this miracle would set in motion a three-year path that would lead to His sacrificial death?

Did Mary comprehend what He was saying? We do not know for sure. Perhaps, at this moment, she recalled the event when, at twelve years old, she found Him in the Temple conversing with the rabbis and discussing profound, spiritual ideas. This incident revealed that He was spiritually engaging and wise beyond His years. She probably never anticipated a time that He would lay down His life because of events that occurred during His lifetime. The wedding feast was a time of celebration not a time for depressing or foreboding thoughts.

The significance of the miracle lies in its symbolism; after all, it is a "sign," pointing to the Messiahship of Jesus. Notice first that there were six water pots, each capable of holding 18-27 gallons. The author draws particular attention to the immense quantity of water. He does so not so much because he is thinking of the amount of purification required during the week of wedding celebration, but because he has in mind the richness of life for those who believe in Jesus. So by using the quantity of these water pots, He is anticipating here how incredibly rich the life of the believer will be.

The water pots had been provided, according to the Mosaic Law, to permit the guests to purify themselves by way of a specifically designated cleansing ritual. However, when writing to illustrate the power of Jesus and thus prove His Messiahship, John regarded the water as representing the Mosaic tradition, the Old Covenant. The number six represented human achievement, incompleteness as in falling short of spiritual perfection; it sometimes possessed a very sinister meaning, even evil itself. If seven was the number for divine perfection and fulfillment, the number six stood for less than perfection, imperfection. No surprise. Six represented the runner who, in spite of intense effort, falls just short of the finish line; it exemplified snatching defeat from the jaws of victory; it often spelled catastrophe. After pondering this event in the life of Jesus, John repurposes this concept to illustrate the fulfillment of Old Testament prophecy.

The six water pots, with their immense quantity of contents, symbolize the inadequacy of Judaism as it awaits the arrival of the Messiah; it represents the imperfect nature of the Law as governed by the Jews. Jesus commands that a servant draw the water from the pots. The word translated "draw" is ἀντλέω (*antleō*) and means to dip or bail out. It is the verb form of the same word used in 4:11 by the woman at the well when she tells Jesus that He has no "bucket" with which to draw water. Here, at the wedding feast, *antleō* infers the use of a seventh vessel representing Christ. This seventh vessel is dipped into one of the pots representing the Mosaic tradition and the imperfection of Judaism. This "drawing out" demonstrates that the Messiah will come out of or arise from within Judaism, not out of any other tradition. So this seventh vessel draws out of Judaism the "new wine" symbolic of the New Covenant. The "good wine" is the wine of the Messiah which is produced by Jesus. Out of the fullness but incompleteness of Judaism, Jesus was "drawn," he emerged. Judaism, with all its ceremonies and godly revelation was not adequate to reveal God in all His glory. Only the incarnation of Jesus is sufficiently powerful to accomplish God's purpose. This "sign," therefore, expresses a powerful declaration that Jesus has come out of the old Jewish tradition to fulfill the Law and the Prophets.

The final words of the headwaiter are significant. For we find suddenly that the new wine, according to his tastes, is superior to the old wine which has been served throughout the week. It was customary at such feasts that the good wine was served first to the guests and, after they had become sufficiently dulled by the good wine, then the host would break out wine of lesser quality. But, alas, not so in this instance. However, it is not the man whose marriage is being celebrated who has withheld the good wine, but God who has now sent His son, the bridegroom, to give life to the world. God gave, at first, the old wine of the Law, without strength, spirit or taste; but according to Galatians 4:4, in the fullness of time He gave the new wine, strong and powerful, fulfilling the Law.

The "miracle at Cana" was the first of seven "signs" about which John writes in his Gospel. This "sign" revealed to a naïve and incredulous Jewish populace that God now "tabernacled" among His people. He had emerged from within the Jewish tradition, according to prophecy, and He now dwelt among His people, prepared to offer them a spiritual rebirth. His glory was present in the form of the man Jesus whose mission would not be fully accomplished until the "hour" of His ultimate glorification.

The Manifestations

The author now sets out to present a series of manifestations which characterize the Messiahship of Jesus. Unlike the "signs" of John, the manifestations do not prove that He is the Christ but offer qualities that point to Him as a Messianic figure. They are infused with the character and spirit of the Messiah and point to a spiritual meaning beyond themselves. The event upon which the first of these manifestations is based occurs within the Temple and in the Synoptic Gospels becomes the catalyst for Jesus' ultimate arrest.

The Cleansing of the Temple, 2:12-22

In order for John to establish the kind of cleansing which the Messiah would bring to the Hebrew nation, he alters the historical position of this incident. Chronologically, then, John consigns this event to a time period that is not consistent with the Synoptics and repurposes it to illustrate the authority of Jesus. By way of the introductory sign in 2:1-11, Jesus has demonstrated His power; now He will assert His authority in a display of His Messiahship.

Jesus enters the Court of the Gentiles as indicated by the use of ἱερόν (*hieron*). The temple noted here was known as "Herod's Temple," located in Jerusalem. It had been under construction for forty-six years. The author places Jesus in the outer courtyard, where financial exchanges from Roman to Jewish money were typically conducted. Observing the degradation of His Father's house, Jesus hastily grabs the nearest whip, a symbol of His authority, and first releases the animals. Probably, at this point, the "changers" themselves have begun to disperse, after which Jesus throws over the tables upon which the money and its associated usury fees are stacked, scattering the money throughout the stalls. Notice that He never struck anyone.

The heart of the incident occurs in vv. 18-21. Jesus has now assumed His Messianic authority as described in Malachi 3:1-3.[18] But the Jewish hierarchy does not

---

18. "'See, I am going to send My messenger, and he will clear the way before Me. Then the Lord you seek will suddenly come to His temple, the Messenger of the covenant you desire—see, He is coming,' says the Lord of Hosts. But who can endure the day of His coming? And who will be able to stand when He appears? For He will be like a refiner's fire and like cleansing lye. He will be like a refiner and purifier of silver; He will purify the sons of Levi and refine them like gold and silver. Then they will present offerings to the Lord in righteousness." (Malachi 3:1-3)

understand His motives. So they ask Him to vindicate His action. To His questioners, Jesus' response to their request seems to be confusing, "Destroy this sanctuary, and I will raise it up in three days." According to them, the "temple" was the physical building in Jerusalem where they worshipped Jehovah. But a closer analysis of the words of Jesus offer quite a different interpretive line. The word "temple" here is not the same word used in v. 14. Jesus employed the Greek ναὸς (*naos*) which, while translated "temple," also refers more specifically to the inner sanctum comprised of the Holy Place and the Holy of Holies. If Jesus is the fulfillment of the Messianic expectation, then His person as the Son of God qualifies Him as the holiest of the holy. He is more than qualified to enter and occupy this inner sanctum of the Temple because His authority is from none other than God the Father.

The words of Jesus in the latter part of v. 19 confounded the Jewish leaders because they did not understand the picture Jesus was painting of His role as the Messiah. ἐγείρω (*egeirō*) commonly meant to awake, rouse or raise up. Rarely was it used to refer to building or construction. When Jesus asserts that He will "raise it up," the Jews interpreted His words to mean that He would "reconstruct" the Temple in three days. John, recalling this event post-resurrection, intensifies the meaning of the response by assigning this particular word to Jesus. It deepened the meaning of the sign by dramatizing the role of Jesus. It referred not so much to the rebuilding of the Temple but the awakening of Jesus from His death experience. However, the Jews never acknowledged their awareness of His meaning and paralleled His words to the Temple in Jerusalem.

None of those who actually witnessed this event, whether disciples, believers or non-believing Jews, fully grasped its meaning or significance. The disciples will understand, eventually, but only after Jesus' death and resurrection, really only after the coming of the Holy Spirit. This cleansing manifestation demonstrated that Jesus not only came with the stamp of God's approval and His authority, but He also came as God, tabernacling among men.

By Jesus' own words, no longer would the Holy of Holies be regarded as the place where sinful man encounters a holy God. Now, Jesus becomes the new meeting place between God and man. No longer will man worship God in the Temple in Jerusalem but in his heart.

Chapter Three

John 2:23 – 4:54

The Offering of New Birth to Israel, 2:23-3:36

The second of the manifestations is the familiar story of Nicodemus, a man with whom Jesus did not trust Himself. A Pharisee, a ruling authority and a member of the honored Sanhedrin, the Supreme Court of Judaism, he is nowhere mentioned in the Synoptic Gospels. In 19:39 we are told that he helped Joseph of Arimathea take down the body of Jesus from the cross and place it in a tomb at significant risk to his well-being and reputation. Otherwise, Nicodemus is an unknown figure.

Nicodemus was not in his position of power because of heredity or influence but because he was wise and possessed a practical yet inquiring mind. His dissatisfaction with the legalism of the Pharisees is vented in his words found in 7:51, words that could flow only from a man of exemplary courage. Nevertheless, he was quite an open-minded individual, and he would not rest until he found the truth. Apparently a man of wealth, he was also a student of the Law. But forthwith, he is "suddenly confronted with the religion of the Spirit."[19]

To this point in his life, Nicodemus had lived by the religion of the Law; now religious culture is changing, ideas are changing, and suddenly there appears a man who seems to be stirring up much trouble by offering a faith that is by Spirit, not by Law. He neither understands the nature of this new, spiritual reality nor does he know whether or not he wishes to be a part of it or conform to it. Nevertheless, he is compellingly confronted with its truth.

Nicodemus sensed, perhaps, that something was being offered here that could not be dismissed as lightly and as easily as his "honorable" colleagues wished. The appearance of this "stranger," he believed, must be investigated firsthand with diligence and care. He was not content to accept secondhand evidence; rather he longed to discern for himself the veracity of Jesus' claims.

His coming by night was probably an indication of caution on his part. He risked significant harm to his reputation and his future by speaking with Jesus. After all, he was a religious leader to whom others looked for guidance and whom they likely would follow. To associate with this man who is obviously "trouble in the making" could cost him everything. He would have approached Jesus clothed in fine purple garb adorned with phylacteries and other accouterments that, to the most casual observer, would have set him apart from the common folk. He would have stood out as a man of power, wealth and influence. So by approaching Jesus at night, he would not have been so easily observed.

The drama of the occasion is how John fashions the narrative—a man of humility contrasted with a man of power. The incident represents the meeting between two

19. Strachan, *op. cit.,* 130.

of Israel's best—a carpenter from Nazareth and a Teacher and Interpreter of the Law. Meeting together, both are descendants of the same nation, yet generations separate them spiritually. Nicodemus was no hypocrite; he was being true to the Law and desired to remain true to the Law. He was a sincere inquirer of the message which Jesus had for Israel.

Since Nicodemus was honest in his query, rather than get lost in the details, Jesus dealt with the core of the question, the Kingdom of God. Entry into the kingdom of God is by being "born from above." The Jews thought the Kingdom of God belonged to them alone by birthright. Jews, and especially the leaders of Judaism, would declare, "We are Jews, God granted the Kingdom to us, and you cannot remove that Kingdom from us. It is ours by birth."

Jesus demolishes this idea. He rather affirms that the Kingdom of God is not an inheritance, rather it is profoundly spiritual, begging that the question in v. 4 be better stated by "how can one whose life and religion are already formed and habitual go back to the beginning?"

Jesus answers that question in vv. 5-6 by saying that it is necessary to fashion a different creature, wholly new, built up in a fresh and Godly way. What is required is a new kind of man. We must be born "from above," reborn. Jesus carefully chooses his words here using γεννηθῇ ἄνωθεν (gennēthē anōthen) to make his point. ἄνωθεν (anōthen) can be variously translated as "from above," "from a higher place," "from the first," "from the beginning," "anew" or "again." No one ever stated this message so impressively as did Jesus. It is a reminder of the prayer in Psalm 51:10: "God, create a clean heart for me and renew a steadfast spirit within me." Could Jesus have been thinking of these words when He spoke to Nicodemus about renewal? Perhaps!

A key component to Jesus' answer is rebirth by "water" and "Spirit." What does Jesus mean introducing the idea of water? The word ὕδωρ (*hudōr*) occurs twenty-one times in the Gospel of John. With the exclusion of this present text, it is used thirteen times to refer literally to water and seven times metaphorically. But to what does it refer in this present context? A variety of answers has been advanced: 1) It is a reference to baptism by the Word, i. e., one is so captivated by the Word that he literally is bathed in it. 2) It refers to the amniotic fluid of physical birth. 3) It is a metaphor referring to the "water" of 19:34 along with the "Spirit." 4) Perhaps it is the baptism of repentance (1:26) which John had been preaching prior to the arrival of Jesus on the scene.

No matter its real significance, Nicodemus did not comprehend the spiritual meaning of Jesus as evidenced by his response. Based upon his rejoinder, one might conclude that Nicodemus understood it to refer to actual physical birth. However, later in his Gospel (7:38) John writes about "living water" which, to the Gospeler, surely symbolizes the Spirit. Not to be discounted is the idea that "water" here may also refer to the "water," representing His Spirit, that issued from the body of Christ at the crucifixion. In this encounter, John portrays Jesus' attempt to employ the commonplace to illustrate the supernatural, but there is also a certain mystery to his declaration, a mystery that Nicodemus did not perceive clearly.

Notice John's continuing emphasis upon the Spirit. Now he introduces another everyday occurrence that Nicodemus would surely understand. Jesus compares the new birth by

Spirit with the wind. The spontaneity of God's Spirit is like the spontaneity of the wind.[20] Like the wind, which makes its presence known by the effect it produces, so the Spirit makes Its presence known by the effects It produces in human lives. By combining these two illustrations, Jesus declares that new birth is by the Spirit alone.

Nicodemus remained confounded by the words of Jesus, so Jesus changes metaphors and compares the earthly to the heavenly in vv. 12-13. "Earthly things" ἐπίγεια (*epigeia*) refers to the Kingdom of God which is God's rule over man in the present age, a kingdom into which men are to enter during their lifetimes on earth by way of spiritual regeneration (rebirth). The assertion of one's faith in Christ encompasses one of these "earthly things." Another assertion is the quality of life lived by the follower of Christ once his faith in Christ has been declared.

The "heavenly things" ἐπουράνια (*epourania*) are those mysteries which no man can declare but which can be made known by the Son of Man who has come down from heaven. These mysteries involve the re-creation of one's spiritual nature and the ultimate union of the Christian with the Father in heaven. They are the mysteries which Jesus declared during His ministry on earth.

How disappointed Jesus must have been with Nicodemus, as he must often be with us. If we are puzzled by and stumble over earthly considerations, issues which can be verified by human experience, how are we to press on to the deeper matters of God, to understand the heavenly?

---

20. Note that the words "wind" and "spirit" are derived from the same Greek word, πνεῦμα (*pneuma*). It can also refer to breath as the breath of God (Genesis 1:2) found in the creation narrative of the LXX.

Albeit somewhat cryptic, Jesus explains His mission on earth in v. 14. Referring to Numbers 21:6f,[21] a passage with which Nicodemus would have been quite familiar, He reasons by comparison. The intent of the comparison is to correlate the healing that came to the snake-bitten Israelites who looked upon the brazen serpent with that of believers who look, with eyes of faith, upon the Son of Man hanging on a cross.[22]

Think of those desperate people, dying in the wilderness by the hundreds, beset by such loathsome creatures from which there was no escape. Yet the word ran through the camp that if only the people would keep their eyes on the brazen serpent lifted up for all to see, there would be deliverance; death would be cheated of its victims.

In contrast Christ points to the cross. Being lifted on that cross of shame, He would deliver believing souls from condemnation. Is it not strange that the voice of a crucified, dying man convinces hearts that God is love? Yet it is upon Calvary, where all seemed lost, that Christ proved to be the most irresistible. Calvary echoes the message that when a person sees Jesus, the heavenly things that appear all dark will dawn clearly. The faithful follower becomes whole, ready to live a fuller, more complete life than ever dreamed possible. Such faith also ushers one into the Kingdom of God.

Within this manifestation contains the "Gospel in a nutshell," John 3:16. One of the most familiar passages in the entire Bible, scholars are divided as to whether these were the actual words of Jesus or an interpretation of the interview of the Gospeler. Does it matter, really? The words are pure truth and capture the substance of the Gospel; they offer a simple, direct assertion of the meaning of the life and death of Jesus and access to the kingdom of God.

---

21. The story of the serpent in the wilderness.
22. Note John 12:32.

And what does entry into the Kingdom provide? Eternal life! This favorite term used by John has little to do with quantity or duration. Rather, it is a qualitative existence which describes not so much the length of a life as the kind of life it is. Eternal life is both present and future. It is present because even here and now we can experience it, if only imperfectly and under earthly limitations. But it also is future because by and by it will widen into a fullness of glory that we cannot as yet begin to comprehend. Nevertheless, whether present or future, eternal life means to put on Christ, to live life after His fashion. It is doing the will of God, more even by far than the abiding forever idea that makes it everlasting.

After responding to the queries of some of his disciples, John once more declares with irrefutable certainty that he is not the Messiah. He then closes this second manifestation with a summary statement in v. 36. Did Nicodemus comprehend and embrace the message of Jesus? John does not state directly, however most scholars are satisfied that he became a believer. John later refers to Nicodemus (7:45-51) when he defends Jesus against a band of chief priests and Pharisees. He also obliquely infers that Nicodemus may have acknowledged the Messiahship of Jesus by mentioning him again (19:38-39) as a part of the crucifixion narrative, having provided myrrh and aloe for Jesus' burial. Perhaps this experience reminded Nicodemus of Jesus' words in 3:14, motivating him to assist Joseph of Arimathea in the burial of Jesus.

Nicodemus would not rest until he found the truth. He wished to understand, and he recognized that Jesus had the answer. After he became a follower, his life was changed forever. Did he continue as a member of the Sanhedrin? In what other respects did his life change? We are not told; that part of the story remains unanswered. From John's later descriptions of him, Nicodemus did not conceal his faith in Jesus. Apparently, for Nicodemus, Jesus became the source of all truth, the meaning of life.

In this encounter Nicodemus represents the greater Israel. Nowhere do we see more clearly Jesus' offer of new birth to Israel than through this conversation with Nicodemus.

Third Manifestation: The Superiority of Christ to the Jewish Fathers, 4:1-42

Because of a growing conflict between Jesus and the disciples of John, Jesus left Judea on His way to Galilee. Unlike most Jews of His time, He chose to take the shortest route by way of Samaria rather than the long route around, avoiding Samaritan soil. Even the disciples were surprised at His decision. It is on this journey that He met the Samaritan woman. Why would He not have traveled the customary route rather going through foreign territory?

John's linguistic approach to describing this story offers no clue regarding the historicity of the encounter. In v. 4 he writes ἔδει δὲ (*edei de*), which has been variously translated as "had to go,"[23] "needed to go,"[24] or "behooved to pass through."[25] The word implies "necessity" or "obligation," begging the question, Why would He have sensed it necessary to go through an area that was commonly both dangerous and so avoided by Jews on racial and cultural grounds? The answer lies in His compulsion to signify that He was the universal Savior who made no distinction between Samaritans and other people. Whether this is Jesus' intent or whether this event actually occurred,

23. New American Standard Version
24. King James Version
25. Wycliffe Bible

we cannot determine, however John used this encounter to declare that Jesus, the universal Messiah, placed no distinction on race or culture but sought that all should find salvation through Him and His death on the Cross.

In order to understand the conversation between Jesus and the Samaritan woman, certain facts about the Samaritans must be made clear. First, they were loyal to the leading principles of Judaism, i. e., they practiced circumcision; they mandated meticulous obedience to the Law; they strictly observed the feasts and the Sabbath. They also held that the Pentateuch[26] was the sole authoritative Scripture by which they were to live their lives. With respect to worship, Mount Gerizim was considered the true sanctuary of the Holy Jehovah. The Jews opposed this belief, deeming the center of worship to be Jerusalem. Eschatologically, their hope was for a "restorer" who was to be similar to Moses, and through his ministry divine favor would be restored to them.

The rarity of this conversation cannot be overstated. A conversation between a man and a woman of this time was unusual enough, but a conversation between a Jew and a Samaritan, given the prejudices of the day, was extraordinary. Jesus was stepping out of His comfort zone and out of the comfort zone of any traditional Jew to speak to this woman. The major reason for such enmity between the Jews and Samaritans lies in the racial makeup of Samaritans. "Samaritan" was the name given to the new, mixed breed (meaning foreign and Jewish) inhabitants whom Esarhaddon (677 BC), the king of Assyria, had brought from Babylon and other places and settled in the cities of Samaria. These people were considered to be foreigners,[27] yet they integrated with the Jews still

---

26. The first five books of the Old Testament.
27. See Luke 17:18.

remaining in the land, often inter-marrying, gradually abandoning their old idolatry and adopting bits and pieces of the Jewish religion. But pure Jews considered them to be defectors of the faith. This woman, therefore, represented her class of people, a people content to live by certain Jewish laws and regulations and not living by others, a renegade or apostate form of Judaism.

When the woman came to Jacob's well for water, Jesus asked her for a drink. This would have been anathema to any pure Jew. He then mentioned a "living water" which the woman would have understood to mean a contrast between fountain or spring water and the still water[28] from Jacob's well. She would have envisioned "living water" to be moving water. Being familiar with the land, she questioned the availability of such water. How could this man offer her a kind of water that was nowhere to be found nearby? Nevertheless, she was willing to receive it in order to relieve her labor of drawing from the well.

The "living water" to which Jesus refers here is spiritual in nature. It represents the Spirit of Jesus offering more than a momentary satisfaction for physical thirst. This idea is more specifically identified in 7:38 where Jesus declares that His Spirit is the "living water." She was thinking on the material level, but Jesus wanted her to think on a spiritual plane, one in which water offered eternal life.

Suddenly, in v. 16 Jesus changes the subject. Why? Maybe He wished to use this occasion to emphasize a special truth. Might John have included this story as actually happening simply to draw attention to Jesus' supernatural knowledge? Or may he have written this story as an allegorical addition to express the history of her people? While it is true that John often took liberty with

---

28. Quiet water as compared to running water in a river, spring or fountain.

chronological timelines, there appears no real evidence to indicate that he concocted stories for the purposes of explaining his thesis. So perhaps he remembers Jesus talking about this encounter, and John employed it to convey a truth about Jesus. There is perchance some truth to both questions. The statement by Jesus, when compared to v. 29, would certainly indicate His supernatural ability. However, He probably used the facts about this woman to reveal the history of her people and the corruption by her people of the Old Testament message.

She is a Samaritan who has been married five times. For John's purposes, her five husbands represent the five gods worshipped by the five nations who were settled in Samaria from Babylon. While scholars have sought to attach spiritual meaning and significance to the number, Jesus is, in truth, a prophet, a "seer," whose knowledge and perception could penetrate to the core and open a new issue for discussion. The number five then possesses little significance other than to represent the facts of her life. The apostasy that she represents is heightened by the fact that her current companion is not her husband. John allows this picture to linger so that he can get on to the lesson of this manifestation.

John then gets to the crux of the issue in v. 20. Worship has to do with real life. It is not some fairy-tale interlude that begins a week of reality. Worship has to do with sin, praise and forgiveness. It is almost as though Jesus says to Himself, "I will show my disciples the kind of worship that my Father seeks and how he seeks it in the midst of real life from the least worthy. She is a Samaritan, a woman, a harlot. Even from an outcast harlot I will show the character of true worship." By focusing attention on the differences in places of worship between the Samaritans and the Jews—a hot topic indeed—John demonstrates that other physical places of worship will be superseded by worship of God in spirit and in truth.

So from Jacob's well to the nature of worship, John included this incident in his Gospel to communicate three truths. He reveals that the salvation offered by Jesus is superior to the salvation claimed by the woman and its superiority is marked by 1) being a gift from God. It is no longer achievable by works of man but as a free gift through the blood of Christ. 2) It is characterized as being a living salvation, a salvation in which one absorbs Christ into his/her life and takes on the Messiah. It is not attained through the strict adherence to rites and rituals, not achieved through one's faithfulness to doctrine and obedience in sacrifice. 3) Salvation is eternal in nature. Eternal refers to the forever presence of Jesus, the spiritual realm in which the Son of God reigns, and those who have accepted Him live an incomparable quality of existence for eternity.

John's takeaway from this experience gives evidence that Jesus is a prophet who can see into the lives of men and can arouse their consciences. He reveals man for what he really is and makes man conscious of his sinful nature.

God is Spirit. In the discussion of the places of worship, Jesus notes that a physical place of worship will no longer be necessary, and He foretells the end of worship on Mount Gerizim and in Jerusalem. Worship will no longer be an outward physical act but an inward spiritual experience.

Most important to John's narrative is the revelation to the Samaritan woman and the readers of this Gospel that Jesus is the Messiah. He is the living water and the embodiment of the Spirit now to be worshipped. Her response manifested a real openness and eagerness to tell someone about the man who had offered a biography of her life. Did she fully understand Jesus' message? Maybe not, because she seemed more astounded that He knew so much about her life than she was enamored by the spiritual message that Jesus spoke. We can assume that the conversation between them included more facts than those John wrote down, because the woman was amazed at how well Jesus knew her life story. Her amazement motivated her to race to the city to proclaim her tale to anyone who would listen.

The writer includes the purpose of this entire incident in v. 42 when he put words into the mouths of those who heard the woman, "We no longer believe because of what you said, for we have heard for ourselves and know that this reality is the Savior of the world."

Pericope, Second Sign, The Faith of a Gentile, 4:43-54

John digresses momentarily to add a pericope (pronounced puh-*rik*-uh-pee) to his narrative. A pericope is a parenthetical statement or a series of statements that form coherent thoughts and functions as a literary unit. As for John's situating this pericope precisely at this point in his Gospel is unknown. The purpose of this parenthetical moment is to underscore the faith of the Gentiles toward Jesus and to offer this event as a second sign of His Messiahship.

Jesus had departed Samaria and Judea, returning to his "own country," v. 44, a phrase referring to Galilee, the area in which Jesus grew to manhood. Although Jesus was born in Judea (Bethlehem), He was raised in the home of Mary and Joseph in Galilee (Nazareth). So apparently He traveled into Galilee so as to prove the general truth that a prophet has no honor in his own country. While it appears somewhat strange to us that John would include this tidbit of information, remember that he views events from the perspective of accentuating the divine sovereignty of the person of Jesus.

The officer whom Jesus encountered in this event may have been attached to the court of Herod Antipas and would have been a Gentile, probably a Roman. There is no evidence that he was attached to any group expressing loyalty to Jesus. He was captivated by the stories he had heard about Jesus from friends he trusted and was sufficiently confident of the miracle-working power of Jesus that he traveled from Capernaum, his base of operation, to Cana in Galilee where he met Jesus. His expression of conviction is clearly illustrated in his courage to commence a journey to contact a man whom both the Jews and the Romans suspected of sedition. He not only put his career on the line, but also, perhaps, even his life.

Jesus appears somewhat reluctant in His interaction with the man because He feared that the officer would be more impressed by His miracles than with His ability to reveal the glory of God through the miracle. Yet, because the officer exhibited compassionate motives, Jesus honored his request.

By this time Jesus is physically spent. He has traveled much and is weary, indicative of His human nature. So by this time, having traveled such distances and finally arriving back in Cana, a request from a Roman officer to journey to Capernaum was not something He wished to entertain at the moment. Jesus takes the opportunity to heal his son at that very moment from that simple, distant place. Strachan notes that "the healing at a distance by Christ's spoken word alone and the father's belief in its power, becomes a true 'sign.'"[29] In what way it reveals the character of God, we are not told. Its intent simply is to offer a "sign" which contrasts the faith of a Gentile and his acceptance of Jesus as Messiah with the rejection of the Jews, His own people.

---

29. Strachan, *op. cit.,* 163.

He is now seen as the Messiah not only for the Jews but also for the people of the world.

In 1:11 John wrote that Jesus came to His own, and they did not receive Him. Jesus wished for His own people, the Jews, to receive Him faithfully as the Son of Man, as the Messiah, the "anointed One." The Jews had long awaited the arrival of the Messiah, but they sought a political, charismatic leader who would guide the future of the Jews as the people of Jehovah.

Jesus has arrived; the Son of Man is walking the earth, and His own people do not recognize or acknowledge His Sonship. In this "sign," John declares with personal conviction that the faith of this Gentile highlights the fact that He has come for all people, not simply the Jews. He is the universal Saviour for all who, in faith, will believe in Him. The value of this "sign" to John's overall message cannot be overstated. Jesus will no longer be identified as the Messiah of the Jews, but He will also be acknowledged as the Messiah of the masses. He will no longer only be the Deliverer of His own people, but He will be the Deliverer of all who believe in His atoning sacrifice on the Cross.

Chapter Four
John 5:1 – 8:50

Third Sign: The Relation of Christ to the Sabbath, 5

John advances his narrative on the Messiahship of Jesus with a third "sign" the purpose of which is to demonstrate the relation of Christ to the Sabbath Day. The "sign" is written in three parts: the miracle itself, vv. 1-9a; the result of the miracle, vv. 9b-16; the interpretation of the miracle, vv. 17-30.

The rabbis in Palestine and the Hellenistic Jews had found in the Genesis account of God resting on the Sabbath a suggestion that at times He ceased His creative activity. They, therefore, advanced the principle that God could do whatever He wanted to do on the Sabbath, and since the whole world was His private residence, He rested. So the logical conclusion would be that man should also rest on the Sabbath.

Jesus came to Jerusalem at a time when the city would have been teeming with revelers at the feast. Did Jesus purposely select this time period to come to Jerusalem? Perhaps. He certainly would have been aware of the crowds He would encounter, and such crowds would offer a distinct opportunity to demonstrate the power of the Father through Him and thus to reveal His Messiahship. Or, His appearance at this time might merely have been a coincidence.

Exactly which feast is being referenced we do not know, but because John is not interested in the accuracy of the historical chronology, it could, perhaps, have been the Feast of Passover or of Tabernacles. Regardless, the streets of Jerusalem were filled with a glut of humanity.

As Jesus strolls the crowded streets, He finds Himself at a popular location of the city, the pool at Bethesda. This pool, acclaimed for its healing powers, attracted many of the infirmed from the region. Probably fed by a spring or artesian aquifer which gushed forth periodically, the ancients anthropomorphized the gushing to actually be the work of an angel who touched or "troubled" the waters. The legend, as passed down through generations, asserted that the first ill or disabled person, then, who entered the water would be healed. Idol worshippers attributed the healing power to a regional divinity which the Jews interpreted to be an angel. The efficacy of such healings is not confirmed or explained.

It was this environment into which Jesus thrust Himself. Determining that it would be an appropriate place to display His power as the Christ, Jesus walks among the maimed and sick and seeks the worst of the worst, a man who had been infirmed for thirty-eight years. In John's Greek text (5:11), Jesus uses seven words to command him to arise, take up his pallet and walk. Could the use of these seven words have significance? In addition to the curative power of Jesus' words, which is evident in the man's physical response, perhaps they reflected the completeness of his healing. Or perhaps they additionally represent the spiritual completeness or fulfillment of Jewish prophecy regarding the Messiah. After all, this is John's sole purpose in writing this Gospel.

With respect to what was forbidden on the Sabbath, the Law was clear. שַׁבָּת (*Shabbat*, Sabbath) was considered to be a pleasant day of respite. The origin of the word is uncertain, but it seems to have originated from the verb meaning to stop, to cease or to keep. For the Jews, its theological meaning is firmly rooted in God's rest following the six days of creation in Genesis 2:2-3.

The purpose of the Sabbath, as written in the Law, was to set aside a time for rest, remembrance, reflection and observance, basic purposes clearly stated in Exodus 20:8 and Deuteronomy 5:12. But the rabbis took these principles considerably farther in the *Mishnah*.

The *Mishnah*, considered to be the cornerstone of Judaism, was redacted early in the third century BC. Its 62 divisions or tractates and six orders provide the backdrop for every subject of Halacha (Jewish law) of the Oral Torah. Its objective was to supplement the oral, and now written, Law and offered distinctive manners of life that would be consistent with the oral tradition. So in the *Mishnah* the rabbis created a litany of restrictions that limited one's activities on the Sabbath to the most basic, so that anyone who so much as carried anything from one domain to another on the Sabbath, was guilty of a violation of the prohibitions for this day.[30] The healing at the Pool of Bethesda occurred on the Sabbath day and was in clear contravention of the rabbinical Law.

As a result of this miracle, Jesus placed Himself in the crosshairs of the priestly elite. Their devotion to the Law was so legalistic that they often put ecclesiasticism and institutionalism above the worth of the individual.

30. See Jeremiah 17:19-27, Nehemiah 13:15-18, Exodus 31:12-17.

In contrast, Jesus' act of compassion not only healed the man of his infirmity, but it also illustrated the power of the living God. Legalism could not accomplish that.

The key to understanding this "sign" is v. 17. Here Jesus said, "My Father is still working, and I am working also." By way of these words Jesus declared that, on earth, He alone is the Son who has the authority of God. He made Himself equal with God.

Though the ecclesiastics looked to the creation event and the seventh day as their premise for resting, they also believed that the creative activity of God had actually never ceased. It was uninterrupted, and since God continued to rest on the seventh day, it would be logical for His people to rest on the seventh day. With that idea in mind, the religionists immediately perceived the heresy of the statement, that Jesus was claiming a sole divine prerogative, making Himself equal with God. Jesus defended Himself by proclaiming that life and judgment (v. 24) had been committed to Him. The Son was able to make alive, and He was also able to judge. Such words and deeds achieved little in reversing the attitudes of the ecclesiastics.

Yes, Jesus works for the good of men on the Sabbath because His Father works on behalf of men on the Sabbath. But this "sign" also revealed how the Father honors the Son, vv. 20-30. The relationship of the Father to the Son is so intimate that the Father has given the Son the power even to raise the dead.[31] However, John is content, at this point, to demonstrate the power of the Son through healing and the superiority of Christ over the oppressive Laws that governed the lives of the Jews of that day. That being accomplished, he moves on.

---

31. John includes v. 25 as a prelude to the raising of Lazarus in which the creative power of God through the Son will be revealed.

Pericope: The Three Great Witnesses, 5:33-41

For the Gospeler, bearing witness was of utmost importance. Consider how often he had employed the word "witness" to this point.[32] Early in his Gospel (1:7), John declared himself to be a witness to the events and "signs" about which he was to write.

To bear witness means to verify, confirm or corroborate the truth of an idea, assertion, or even the genuineness of a person's character or his or her declaration of spiritual reality. During the first century, a single witness could offer a modicum of corroboration, but legal proof in cases of serious or grievous complaints required at least two witnesses; three might even offer greater confirmation.[33]

To discourage doubt in the veracity of His claim as the Son of God, Jesus offers the testimony of three witnesses. The first He declares to be that of John whose preaching the Jews heard and many heeded, but now they considered his preaching, his announcement of Jesus as the Christ and his close relationship with Jesus as a disciple, as abandonment of his Jewish heritage. Nevertheless, the Gospeler knows the heart of the Baptist and summons the skeptics to hear his witness on behalf of Jesus.

The second is the witness of the Father Himself. His witness is manifested in two forms. There is the "work" of the Father through the Son that bears witness to the truth of Jesus' assertion. Jesus points to the miracles, the "signs," as testimony of His claim, a testimony bearing greater witness even than that of John, His Forerunner. The second witness of the Father considers the manner

---

32. 1:7; 1:8; 1:15; 3:11; 3:26; 3:28
33. Based upon Deuteronomy 19:15.

of His voice, His words. The authenticating voice of the Father bears witness to the fact of Jesus' Messiahship. His baptism and the appearance of the dove offer heavenly evidence of Jesus' spiritual connection with the Father. Yet the ecclesiastics dismiss the work and voice of the Father by rejecting the words, work and ministry of Jesus.

Finally, the Scriptures themselves bear witness to Jesus as the Christ. The Jews had read the ancient words of the prophets, the bards of ancient times, v. 39, and yet did not harken to their deep value. Their stubbornness and their reluctance to see the fulfillment of those Scriptures blinded their eyes to the reality of Jesus' claim. Yet the Scriptures did, indeed, bear witness to Him.

John closes this chapter in the saga (vv. 41-47) by indicting the Jews in a most severe manner. He charges them with lacking in love, deficient in the love of God which can bring salvation and offer eternal life. They are a spiritual vacuum, absent the power that only God can provide. They will not even receive Jesus when He comes in the name of God. They consider Him a blasphemer and worthy of scorn. While Jesus appeals to them to look to His works as evidence of God's power in Him, they rather ignore the "signs" because they have not discerned the true meaning of those "signs." They are blinded to the truth.

Most apparent is the desire of the rabbis to seek the glory of men rather than the evidence of God's approval, v. 44. The rabbinic "patting on the back" of each other as a sign of honor was more important to their spiritual gratification than the truth of God. Their spiritual immaturity led them to disregard the truth standing before them in the person of Jesus in favor of human satisfaction and personal glory.

Fourth Sign: Christ as the New Manna from Heaven, 6:1-71

Christ is the "new manna" from heaven. Manna was a physically sustaining commodity for the Jews as they wandered in the wilderness, but, as illustrated by this "sign," Jesus becomes a spiritually sustaining commodity to those who accept His Messiahship and trust His atoning death on the cross.

As the new manna, Christ is identified as the Bread of Life. John's account actually comprises all of chapter six and consists of two sections, with one section serving as an introduction to a section of extensive interpretive discourse in vv. 22-71.

The background for this "sign" encompasses two elements. The first element is the giving of the manna to the Israelites in the wilderness following their release from Egypt (Exodus 16:4). The second element is the movement of the crowd from the sea where Jesus fed them over to Capernaum. The curiosity of the crowd, after witnessing the miracle, was sufficiently intense as to cause them to seek out Jesus and follow Him wherever He went. He was not interested in their curiosity, only their understanding of who He was. They found Him on the other side of the sea at Capernaum and followed Him there.

The multitude was drawn to the shores of the sea because they had seen Jesus heal the sick and afflicted. Not unlike today, people were fascinated with the extraordinary, the rare, the different. So their fascination grew even as a common allure for the unusual grows with no real vitality or saving interest. They sought no change in their spiritual condition. They were on the seashore because they had followed Him there, had seen Jesus perform other fascinating miracles and they wished to see Him perform others.

Notice in v. 5 that Jesus actually precipitated the problem. This crowd had been following Him all day, and it was past time for a meal, so He inquires of His disciples what they should do to satisfy the crowd's need for nourishment. Andrew, the "go to guy" among the disciples, solves the problem, vv. 8-9, by finding a small boy with a lunch that had been prepared by his mother. The rest of the story is commonly known.

The food that Jesus offered that day is a "type" or symbol for the manna provided to the children of Israel in the wilderness. Just as Jesus becomes like the bronze serpent, offering life, so the loaves and fishes, like the manna, represent spiritual food available only through the blood of Christ to those who faithfully trust Him.

After feeding the five thousand, twelve baskets of fragments were collected. These twelve baskets symbolized the twelve tribes of Israel or the old manna provided by Jahweh in the wilderness. The people whom Jesus fed this old manna represented the Old Israel. Conversely, Jesus, taking the loaves and fishes and multiplying them, provides a new kind of manna, a spiritual sustenance of eternal quality, a new kind of covenant, by fulfilling God's promise in the Old Testament.

The result of this miracle was the attempt, by the crowd, to proclaim Jesus as a prophet, the Messiah they had awaited. But they proclaimed Him to be a Jewish Messiah, not a Christian Messiah. They wished to take Him, by force if necessary, and make Him a king. Sensitive to their plan, Jesus would have nothing to do with it. He withdrew to get away from the crowd and to pray for power from the Father, wisdom to know what to do and the courage and willingness to follow through with the Father's plan.

The discourse of vv. 22-25 is only intended to provide an historical link with the event that has preceded the discourse, i. e., the feeding of the five thousand. John is seeking to account for the presence of the crowd again on the other side of the lake. However, it is important to note that the Gospeler is not really concerned with the exact manner by which the crowd crossed. His sole purpose is to make plain that the people who were miraculously fed on the seashore are the same audience to whom the discourse on the bread of life is directed at Capernaum.

Introduction to the "I AM" Sayings and the Interpretation of The Fourth Sign

The interpretation of this fourth "sign" is written in vv. 26-71. In vv. 26-40 Jesus initiates the discourse about the bread of life. In so doing, He introduces the first of His seven great "I AM" sayings in the Gospel of John. The number, seven, of these sayings was not lost on John, rather he included them to show the perfect fulfillment of the mission of Him who issued the sayings. If one were to combine the "I AM" sayings with the "signs" of the Christ as a single tome, one would have the entire Gospel in a single abbreviated form. These two elements of John's Gospel are the purest form of God's promise fulfilled in Jesus Christ.

A form of this phrase occurs forty-five times in this Johannine work either in a direct nominative or direct metaphorical reference. Throughout the Gospel other oblique references to Jesus as "I AM" can be found but are more indirect in their orientation. The seven designated "I AM" sayings of Jesus are characterized by the inclusion of the Greek ἐγώ εἰμί (*egō eimi*), "I am." The inclusion of ἐγώ (*egō*) in John's text makes this phrase emphatic, and it is only the genuine "I AM" sayings of Jesus that include the Greek ἐγώ (*egō*). John employs the grammatically emphatic form in these "I AM" sayings to confirm that Jesus is declaring Himself unmistakably to be equal with God.

The direct nominative reference infers the addition of the pronoun "he," and is found in such passages as 4:26, "I am He, the One speaking to you." The "*He*" is not a part of the original text but is inferred from the context of the sentence. Another example would be found in 18:6, "When He told them, 'I am *He*', they stepped back and fell to the ground." Again the "*He*" is not part of the original text but is implied and forms a nominative use.

The second kind of "I AM" citations comprise the direct metaphorical references, that is, they are employed in conjunction with a similitude. They form a picture that is closely related to the event or occasion to which Jesus is connected. These references can be found in what have become known as the great "I AM" sayings of Jesus. Passages such as the present one serves as an initial example of one of these great "I AM" passages. Here the "Bread of Life" forms the similitude with which the "I AM" saying is associated. Or 8:12, where Jesus declares, "I am the light of the world." What marvelous portraits these sayings paint of the Messiah!

These direct metaphorical usages of this phrase can be traced to Exodus 3:14 where God encountered Moses at the burning bush. The Old Testament name of God derives from the verb "I AM" or "I will be" and denotes a bond between the name and the being itself. "Jahweh is the Source of all being and has Being inherent in Himself. Everything else is contingent Being that derives existence from Him. The name bespeaks the utter transcendence of God. God is beyond all predications or attributes of language. He is the source and foundation of all possibility of utterance and thus is beyond all definite descriptions."[34]

34. www.hebrew4christians.com.

The God (יהוה, Jahweh, "I AM WHO I AM") who offered physical salvation by safely bringing the children of Israel out of Egyptian bondage has once again brought salvation in the form of His Son who is the human essence of the "I AM." Jesus' declaration offers assurance that He and the Father, the Great "I AM" of the Old Testament, are one.

As a result of this fourth "sign" three conclusions may be drawn. First, Jesus verifies that He is, indeed, the Bread of life (v. 35). Only He can completely satisfy the hunger of one's soul, yet the Jews continue to seek a Messiah that satisfies physically. Alfred Plummer wrote, "The superiority of Christ to the manna consists in this, that while it satisfied only bodily needs for a time, He satisfies spiritual needs forever."[35]

As the manna that satisfies spiritually, He satisfies completely (v. 35). Indeed, He rejects none whom the Father sends to Him (v. 37), and He will lose nothing of the divine character with which the Father has endowed Him as His Son (v. 39). His mission is solely to do the will of the Father and to that mission He is firmly dedicated.

Second, Jesus reveals Himself as the true Passover lamb. Look at vv. 52-59 where He all but institutes the Lord's Supper in words that the crowd does not understand. This precursor to the Lord's Supper, the actual institution of which does not appear in John's Gospel, is so preternatural and intrepid as to leave the crowd wondering what He was really saying. Their actions, as written in the subsequent verses, expose their lack of understanding.

Third, the "sign" discloses the spiritual perception of the disciples, both those who were following Him and the Twelve (vv. 59-71). Like sifting wheat, Jesus' words cause such discomfort to many of His followers that they abandoned Him at this point because He was not what they

35. Plummer, *op. cit.,* 150.

thought Him to be (v. 66). Whether disillusionment, paucity of insight or simple loss of interest, the crowd departed, leaving only the Twelve Disciples.

What are the lessons to be learned from this "sign"? We learn that Jesus is the Bread that can sustain us forever spiritually, providing eternal life. We learn that the human Jesus without the incarnation is futile. We learn that false disciples will go away, will abandon a spiritual nature in favor of physical satisfaction. We learn that true disciples realize that Jesus is the Holy One of God and stay with Him because their eyes of faith have perceived His true nature.

Fourth Manifestation: Christ in the Temple, the Teacher of Israel, 7:1-52

In this fourth manifestation, Jesus reveals Himself as the great teacher of Israel. The setting for this encounter, the Temple, is most fitting, and vv. 1-11 provide a background or timeframe of preparation for the time when Jesus will appear in the Temple. The time of year was the Feast of Tabernacles, also referred to as the Feast of Booths. Originally a harvest festival, it had become associated with the deliverance of the Jews from Egypt.

John appears to have skipped six months of Jesus' ministry "because the Jews sought to kill Him and for most of these six months Jesus withdrew from Galilee."[36] Was He inclined to return to public life? Certainly not at this time. Mistakenly His brothers perceived that Jesus wished to become a public figure, and they encouraged Him to attend the feast and make Himself known as a public figure, to seek the adulation of the people, not from the perspective of His Messiahship but simply for being a famous person.

---

36. Robertson, *op. cit.,* 76.

Could this suggestion have been the result of His brothers' skepticism? The Gospeler writes in v. 5 that "for not even His brothers believed in Him." Perhaps they believed in His power—after all they had seen Him in action performing miracles—but they did not understand why He would wish to remain little known and unassertive. So as Jesus faced rejection from large groups of followers, He now must face prejudice within His own family circle.

Jesus' response to His brothers is reminiscent of His words to His mother in Cana, "My time has not yet arrived." His use of Ὁ καιρὸς (*ho kairos*) is appropriate to His mission and parallels ὥρα (*hōra*) in 2:4. While καιρὸς (*kairos*) is translated "time," it can also mean a "fitting opportunity," a "quality of time" or a "unique moment in time." In contrast to χρόνος (*chronos*) which describes a definite period or chronological time, καιρὸς (*kairos*) refers to suitable circumstances. Jesus sensed that the time for the public revelation of His Messiahship was quickly approaching, including His crucifixion, but that time had not yet come.

Notice that, after some time had past but before the conclusion of the Feast, Jesus secretly enters the city, vv. 10-13. Beginning with v. 14 Jesus deliberately asserts His authority as a Teacher in the Temple. When questioned about His credentials, Jesus responded in vv. 16-18 by claiming to be a Teacher sent from God. Such blasphemy! He has now publicly opened Himself to coarser criticism. He even asks the crowd, "Why do you want to kill Me?"

In response Jesus argues that His right to "break" the law is more valid than the assumed right of these religious leaders, essentially His enemies, to enforce the law. He follows this question with a reference to the healing of the man at the Pool of Bethesda, an event that had occurred perhaps a year and a half earlier in the chronological life of Jesus (5:1-9). He argues, querying them as to whether it is better to heal or to harm on the Sabbath. He had healed a man on the Sabbath day, but they were willing to "break" the law on the Sabbath by performing a ceremonial circumcision and taking a part of a man's body. His intention, though misconstrued by the crowd, was to show that a person is more important than an institution.

Jesus continued to teach in the Temple, declaring His relationship with the Father and proclaiming a message that made Him equal with God. To His listeners, His words were blasphemy, sheer heresy.

Jesus' words in vv. 37-38 were especially perplexing, but He continued to teach, and the people murmured and became restless in what they heard, vv. 40-52. Why were His words so sacrilegious, especially to the Jewish leadership and teachers of the Law?

The Feast of Tabernacles was coming to a close. Each day, during the Feast, a priest would go to the pool of Siloam and draw a vessel of water that was ceremonially poured over the altar. Its purpose was to call the favor of God upon the growing season by bringing life-giving rains. Now Jesus uses the water allegory to refer to Himself.

Water is not only a life-sustaining element, but in the Old Testament it is a symbol of the Spirit. Here Jesus refers to the water-pouring of the Feast and points to Himself as the source of water that will end one's thirst forever. The rabbinical teachings of the Jews were "that the Holy Spirit had departed from Israel when the last of the prophets, Zechariah and Malachi, had died. They looked for a fresh outpouring in the Messianic age."[37] Jesus was declaring here and now that He was that "fresh outpouring."

---

37. Strachan, *op. cit.,* 203.

Pericope, 7:53-8:11

Beginning in 7:53 we encounter yet another parenthesis of thought. It is generally accepted by scholars that this passage does not originally belong to this Gospel.[38] Its introduction may have served as an illustration of the idea of Jesus as Judge. Whatever the reason, the Feast of Tabernacles is concluding and the visiting throngs are leaving the city. And as He is often want to do, Jesus once again goes to the Temple (8:2).

His time of solitude is interrupted by a group of people who bring a woman who had been caught in the act of adultery. Their motive for bringing this woman before Jesus was less than spiritual in nature. They rather wished to put Him in a position of agreeing or disagreeing with Moses. Having already referred to the Law of Moses in 7:19, 22 and 23, Jesus sensed their real motivation.

John surely includes this encounter to show that the legalism of the Law and the Pharisees who interpreted that Law cannot coexist with love, a combination which represents a stark contrast between the Law of the Old Testament and the New Revelation in Jesus. Through this experience Jesus is seen as superior to Moses. He is also considered to be the compassionate Jesus in His non-judgmental attitude toward her.

What did He write on the ground? History does not reveal the specific character of the writings. Perhaps it was a list of the sins of her accusers, perhaps her own

38. E.g., Alfred Plummer, *The Gospel According to St. John*, Wilbert F. Howard's exegesis in *The Interpreter's Bible*, and A. T. Robertson, *The Divinity of Christ*. Hoskyns, T*he Fourth Gospel*, 563, states that "in the Greek Codices Sinaiticus and Vaticanus, and in the Washington and Koridethi manuscripts, the text of the Fourth Gospel runs continuously from 7:52 to 8:12, without any sign of a break."

sins. Or maybe he was simply doodling in the dirt, offering time for them to ponder what they were about to do. In any case, the emphasis for the Gospel writer was the fact THAT Jesus wrote in the sand, not what was actually written. Here is engaged the sinless Son of God confronting a group of powerful Jews who wished to carry out the Law as prescribed. But Jesus observed a more loving and persuasive approach to this woman. The departure of her accusers confirms His divine insight.

As Jesus lifts His head and sees that her accusers have left, He repeats words reminiscent of 3:17. He has not entered this world to judge or condemn, and He will not judge or condemn this woman. Jesus has come to release the transgressor from the penalty of sin. Nowhere are His grace and mercy better illustrated than here.

Not only did Jesus not condemn her, He wanted to release her from the penalty of sin. Note His admonition to her in v. 11. "Do not sin anymore" is a translation of the Greek πορεύου καὶ μηκέτι ἁμάρτανε (*poreuou kai mēketi hamartane*), "Go, and from now on do not sin anymore." The verb "sin" is a present imperative of ἁμαρτάνω (*hamartanō*), "to sin." The present tense indicates that this woman may, perhaps, have been a local prostitute or a woman of iniquitous reputation. The form of the verb here refers to action that is continual, habitual. Jesus counsels this woman, yea, admonishes her, to cease her habit of sinning. He has now changed this woman's life; He has changed her perspective. Her view of life now is not one of actively seeking to sin because that had apparently been her lifestyle. She had made it a habit of sinning; she had sought out sin as a way of life, as a style of life. Jesus said, "Don't do that any more."

Fifth Manifestation: Christ as the Light of the World, 8:12-30

John's fifth manifestation begins in verse 12 where he introduces a series of controversial teachings of Jesus. The first of these teachings comprises vv. 12-20, where we encounter the second of the "I AM" sayings of Jesus. Here, Jesus presents Himself as the Light of the World. Light, like life, in John's Gospel, always possesses a principled element, that is, its effect is fundamental to spiritual survival.

The basis for the Johannine concept of light is utterly Jewish. Such is illustrated both in canonical Old Testament passages such as Isaiah 60, Psalm 27:1 and Proverbs 6:23. But the idea is also found in Rabbinical writings as well. Light, in Hebrew thought, is regarded as a synonym for salvation.[39] And so Jesus' use of the idea of light here is yet another revelation, yes, even a pronouncement that He Himself is Saviour and Messiah. Notice that Jesus did not orally declare Himself to be the Messiah, but He obliquely described Himself as such through the use of this phrase. His use of "light" reminds us of the creation story, a reference that was probably not lost on those who heard Him and which created either confusion or antipathy.

Jesus startlingly stirred a controversy by His words, "where I'm going, you cannot come." These words, which form the theme of this section, are typically interpreted to refer to Jesus' death when His work on earth would have been accomplished, and He would be going to the Father. Notice the re-emphasis of the "I AM" statements in v. 28, a direct nominative reference, not one of the seven recognized "I AM" statements of John. His assertion affirms His deity and by being lifted up, He will be exalted by the Father. Truly the fulfillment of this statement will

---

39. Strachan, *op. cit.*, 205-206.

be recognized by many people once He has been crucified. But, for now, v. 30 indicates only that many "believed in Him" because of the authority of His speech.

Freedom and Truth, 8:31-50

Jesus provokes yet a third controversy which focuses on the idea of freedom. Jesus is shown as the messenger of the New Covenant who confers the kind of freedom that Abraham could not give. The freedom about which Jesus speaks is freedom from the slavery of sin and such freedom is characterized by three elements:

1. Abiding in Jesus—an essential feature of discipleship. Jesus becomes the dwelling place of the believer, and the believer takes on the characteristics of Him in whom he rests. Jesus "tabernacles" in the believer as the believer abides in the spirit of Christ.

2. Those abiding in Jesus will know the truth. "You will know the truth," said Jesus, "all truth." No longer will you be in darkness, but the light of truth will abide in you because Jesus is the controlling factor in your lives.

3. Those abiding in Jesus will be free from the burden of sin. "And the truth shall set you free," Jesus said. Freedom on earth might be relative in nature, but freedom in Jesus is to be "free indeed," v. 36, truly free.

Sin is a debasing, demoralizing and dehumanizing delusion which lurks in the darkest recesses of the human spirit. Truth, like light, exposes the delusion of darkness, bares the bonds of malevolence and frees the spirit of man from the ruthless chains of lawlessness and unrighteousness. This kind of freedom is to be "free indeed"!

Jesus never avoided a controversy. While He also did not engender discord deliberately, He often created it by virtue of His message. And so another dispute is created in vv. 58-59.

Surely He realized that what He was about to say would be an abomination to His listeners. The idea of pre-existence was anathema to the Jews; they could not conceive of the idea. Here Jesus offers another statement in which He implicitly contends to speak in the name of the eternal wisdom of God, to speak as the *logos*. Although written as ἐγώ εἰμί (*egō eimi*), it is in the direct nominative form and is not considered to be one of the seven "I AMs" of John. Nevertheless, the statement did serve its purpose in this context. By making this "bizarre" statement, He claimed to share His divine place as Mediator between God and man with none other than Father Abraham.[40] Jesus is thus forced to leave the Temple surreptitiously and hide from those who would have stoned Him because His "hour had not yet come" (8:20).

---

40. Strachan, *op. cit.,* 216.

and light of the world. The scene of this fifth "sign" is still Jerusalem and the concluding time for the Feast of Tabernacles. The disciples' question in v. 2 reflects the culture's most common ideas with respect to the relationship between physical suffering and sin. The theology and popular doctrine of the times postulated that not only all suffering in this life was the direct result of sin and its interference with our natural interactions with God, but sin also triggered such negative conditions as natural disasters. Much of this thought found its source in the transmigration of the soul in which the soul of a man, as a consequence of sin, might be forced to pass into other bodies and be punished there. In spite of the descriptive agony of Job's protest in their own Scriptures, these disciples assumed instinctively that this man's blindness from birth was a result of sin, either his own or that of his parents.

The major purpose in including this story in the Gospel narrative is twofold. First, it is included to provide an opportunity to manifest the power of God. By this miracle, both physical and spiritual healing become the purview of God's power. Second, the story serves to introduce the symbol of the Good Shepherd which begins in 9:35 and continues into chapter 10.

Notice several elements and symbols in this story:

1. Jesus kneels on the ground and forms a paste of clay and spittle. Why? The spittle serves as a symbol of the inner life of Jesus given forth. It represents, in a sense, a prophecy of Jesus' sacrifice in which He gives of Himself to save others. Here he offers up a part of Himself (spittle) to heal a blind man just as He will give up all of Himself to bring spiritual healing to our lives.

2. Jesus encourages the man's own participation in the healing process by telling him to go and wash in the pool of Siloam. By obeying, the man witnessed to his own healing experience.

3. The religious leaders, motivated by envy or religious distraction, object to Jesus' actions in general but most especially because He performed this miracle on the Sabbath day. These ecclesiastics tried to find every reason possible to trap Jesus, to charge Jesus with fraudulence because of some action of His that they do not condone. As a result, they not only call the man's blindness into question, but they also excommunicate him, v. 34.

The man born blind is considered by John as a "type" of Israel. His blindness, according to the words of Jesus, was to provide the Messiah an opportunity to demonstrate His power and authority. As Jesus opened the eyes of the blind man to the light, so He offered Light to His own people, even those who refused to accept the Light offered.

Theology played no role in the blind man's initial reaction to the miracle. His discussion with the Jewish leaders only confounded them because he could produce no plausible explanation for his restoration of sight except to describe what Jesus did. The now sighted, formerly blind man could only respond with respect to the fact that he was once blind and could now see. He did not add a theological explanation to his response.

The Jewish leaders were not satisfied with this man's answers to their queries. Feeling threatened by the growing popularity of Jesus, these false shepherds are faced with a dilemma. After repeatedly querying the blind man, they ask among themselves, "What do we do with this man who is delusional?" They have several choices, and chief among them is excommunication.

Jewish excommunication took three forms. The mildest form was simply a "rebuke," in which the person was prohibited from entering the synagogue for 7-30 days. A second form was a "thrusting out" form of excommunication which could last 30 days or longer, depending upon the gravity of the offense. Permanent exclusion described the final form of excommunication. The offender could never enter the synagogue and never participate in official Jewish ceremonies. Further, he lost his livelihood and was banned from any kind of social interaction. He was even treated as dead to his family and his people. This man suffered permanent exclusion.

Jesus Asserts His Deity, 9:35-41

For the third time in the Gospel Jesus definitively declares His divine nature as the "Son of Man."[41] Now Divine assurance is within the reach of this formerly blind man. Once confronted with the words of Jesus declaring His deity, the man confesses his sins and accepts the notion that Jesus is, in fact, the Son of Man, v. 38. The man had heard the title, now he had experienced firsthand the reality of the revelation. His life was changed, his sight restored and his new life in Christ began. His journey with Jesus has taken him from historical fact to hallowed faith.

Sixth Manifestation: Christ as the Good Shepherd of Israel, 10:1-21.

With Jesus' declaration in 9:37, He reveals Himself as the True Shepherd of Israel. Now He progresses a step

---

41. Other declarations of His deity occurred in 4:26 and 8:28.

farther and offers a definitive account of The Good Shepherd to illustrate His meaning, vv. 1-5. The Good Shepherd story has often been described as a parable of Jesus. The word John employs in v. 6 is παροιμίαν (*paroimian*), which refers to a proverb, allegory or figurative saying,[42] and whose real significance and purpose are somewhat elusive and require interpretation.

This interpretation of the "figure of speech"[43] follows in vv. 6-18. Jesus reveals Himself once again as the Son of Man by using the image of a sheepfold door. The "I AM" of v. 7 constitutes yet another of the great "I AM" sayings of Jesus in John. These words of Jesus are a fitting prelude to His ultimate assertion as "the way" (14:6).

Take notice that John paints this word picture in three representations. The first representation, vv. 1-5, pictures the typical door of the sheepfold. While this same image is repeated in vv. 7-9, these verses also include the declaration that Christ is, figuratively, the door of the sheepfold. Finally, between vv. 9 and 11, John pens an interlude of sorts which he uses to link the segments together.[44] In v. 11, Christ is revealed as the Good Shepherd.

The backdrop of this portrait is the ancient occupation of sheep herding. At evening, shepherds would collect their sheep into a common fold surrounded by pickets and walling material. Only one door was provided for entrance and exit. Once the shepherd's flock entered the enclosure, the shepherd was free to leave since the sheep would be guarded by a gatekeeper. If no one were available to guard the sheep or serve as gatekeeper, the shepherd would place his body across the entrance to insure that the sheep would not wander from the enclosure during the night without

42. Joseph Henry Thayer, *Greek-English Lexicon of the New Testament*, Grand Rapids: Zondervan Publishing House, 1962, 460.

43. Note: These are the words of the *New American Standard Bible*.

44. Plummer, *op. cit.,* 216.

means to satisfy a dilemma in which they find themselves. They could not explain Jesus' conduct over the past months, and they were puzzled and their minds confused.

Jesus provides an answer that offers keen insight into the relationship between the True Shepherd and His sheep. He specifies five characteristics of the sheep and the shepherd in vv. 26-29.

1. The sheep hear and recognize His voice, v. 27. They will follow no other master, not be distracted by the cacophony of the world. Every follower of Christ acknowledges His words, cherishes His sacrifice and lives obediently.

2. The Good Shepherd knows and values His own sheep, v. 27. He knows the hearts and minds of His people, and He embraces them with a divine love that is unparalleled.

3. The sheep will follow the True Shepherd, v. 27. Because Christians have faith and trust in the words of Jesus, they are obedient to Him and follow Him wherever that journey may take them.

4. The True Shepherd gives them eternal life, v. 28. He offers assurance of a life that is less characterized by unending time than by the quality of time because of the divine presence of the Shepherd.

5. The Good Shepherd will not allow one of His sheep to perish, vv. 28-29. What a promise! Sin cannot defeat those who claim the Good Shepherd as leader, and His eternal presence awaits them after death. Death, as difficult as it is for us, is ultimate healing because it ushers us into the very presence of the Father. And we are in His presence forever.

The Jews are now more perplexed than ever. Because Jesus has once more declared His divinity (v. 30), they take up stones to kill Him. But alas! Jesus is ready.

Nowhere in the New Testament is Jesus' keen intellect more evident than in vv. 34-38. Perceiving that they wished to trap Him so that they might destroy Him, He quotes from their own Scriptures, Psalm 82:6 (v. 34). The tables are now turned. They want a plain, yes or no answer; He offers a conundrum. Yet, while His answer offers no more "proof" than they already possessed, they could not stone Him as they had wished for want of a legal reason. After all, His "hour" had not yet come.

Sixth Sign: Christ as the Great Giver of Life, 11:1-46

To this point John has described miraculous events that point inexorably to the Messiahship of Jesus. What more powerful means could John employ as a "sign" of the Christ than to select an occurrence involving life and death. This is not some transient event in the life of Christ, something He stumbled upon or an occasion that arose by happenstance. This was an event of intentionality.

Some scholars like James Drummond call into question the actual historicity of this miracle.[47] By its absence from the Synoptic Gospels, they would declare it simply as an allegory to reveal the fulfillment of prophecy. It is John's way of proving a preconceived notion. Nevertheless, the best argument for its authenticity is offered by A. T. Robertson, "If Jesus is the Logos made flesh (chapter 1), the Son of God with power over life and death as He claimed (chapter 5),

---

47. James Drummond, *An Inquiry into the Character and Authorship of the Fourth Gospel,* New York: Charles Scribner's Sons, 1904, 62-63.

why could He not do what God can do?"[48] If Jesus is, in fact God, then He has the power to perform this miracle as He did any other miracle.

Scholars who deny that this miracle actually occurred do so by assuming that it did not fit the narratives of the Synoptic Gospels and so was not included therein. John, however, witnessed beyond the historical event to interpret its spiritual meaning and its value as an identifier of Jesus as the Christ.

So here in the eleventh chapter the sixth of the series of "signs" is described. This "sign" distinguishes, more than all of the others to this point, that Jesus was the supreme gift of the *logos* to men, the First Principle, offered from the Father to give New Life to sinful man. Underlying this "sign" is the universalistic element in the power of Jesus to revive life. Once again this great giver of life engages in an act which ultimately and finally leads to His own death.

Consider the miracle like a drama with four acts.[49] It takes place under four separate circumstances. The first act consists of the report on the death of Lazarus and is described in vv. 1-6. This family, located in Bethany, a small town less than two miles from Jerusalem, was not unknown to Jesus. He had likely visited the home of this family on other occasions. Luke 10:38-42, for example, tells the story of one encounter of Jesus with this family which may, perhaps, have occurred earlier than this contact. He knew them all and not just informally but intimately. The family consisted of Mary, the spiritual seeker, the sensitive sister, the inquisitive one; Martha, the doer, the organizer, the busy one; and Lazarus. This being the only reference

---

48. Robertson, *op. cit.*, 90.
49. Strachan identifies each section as a "scene."

to Lazarus,[50] nothing is known of his life except his family relationships. Lazarus has died, and Jesus tarries. Why?

Jesus was aware of the danger He faced at that moment. His reputation had been cemented, and there were overtures in the planning stages to do Him harm. Jesus was aware of those dangers if He returned to this area. It was not safe for Him. After the encounter with the Jews in chapter 10, he withdrew to an area "across the Jordan to the place where John had been baptizing earlier" (10:40). It is not immediately obvious to the reader where Jesus was staying, but apparently Mary and Martha knew.

John indicates that Jesus already sensed that Lazarus had died because He had heard that Lazarus was sick and He stayed two days later. Perhaps His postponement lay in His knowledge of the plans of the Jewish leaders. So why put Himself in danger now when His "hour" had not yet come? Furthermore, His delay in arriving on scene both taught patience to those who waited for Him to come and offered an opportunity for the glorification of the Son of God.

Jesus knew what was about to happen. Mary and Martha learned a valuable lesson as a result of this miracle—be patient. But they also witnessed the glorification of Jesus in this event. So He delayed His departure for two days so that He might work the supreme miracle of raising Lazarus from the dead.

Act 2 begins two days later. In vv. 7-16 His disciples attempt to restrain Him from going to Bethany because of the danger it posed to Him physically. To the disciples' remonstrations, Jesus replies rather poignantly in vv. 9f with a proverb referring to the length of the day. Its meaning, while perplexing to the disciples, was firmly fixed in the mind of Jesus. As Hoskyns has noted, "As men journey

50. The only other reference to Lazarus is later in 12:9-10.

securely through the twelve hours of the day when the sun shines, but stumble in the night when the light is removed, so the work of the Son of God must be accomplished in the allotted time."[51] Then in v. 14, Jesus not only perceives that Lazarus has, indeed, died, but He also declares the same in no vague or ambiguous terms.

Now the time has come, that καιρός (*kairos*), that fitting time, that moment in time designated for a specific purpose (7:6). The raising of Lazarus and the passion of the Christ are inescapably connected. This act of kindness and power will inevitably motivate the Jewish leaders to take deadly action against Jesus. It becomes the "last straw."

Act 3, vv. 17-32, begins with the arrival of Jesus at the home of Mary and Martha. Lazarus has now been in the grave for four days, an important fact with respect to the miracle. Strack and Billerbeck recount the Jewish beliefs of the day when they write that, according to certain forms of Jewish culture the soul was regarded as having departed the body after three days. The mourning of the family and friends then reached its climax on the third day. For each of those three days, it was believed that the soul would return hoping that it might re-inhabit the body. But if it saw that the fashion of its face had changed, then it departed once more and forsook the body forever. Mourning, therefore, reached its climax on that third day, the day on which the body would have reached a point of significant decomposition and all hope of any restoration to life by what have been considered natural means was banished. At this point, resuscitation could only be accomplished by a new and creative act of God. Jesus became the source of that act.[52]

---

51. Hoskyns, *op. cit.*, 400.
52. Strack and Billerbeck, *op. cit.*, 544.

The focal passage of this third act is v. 25 in which Jesus declares yet another of the "I AM" sayings. This saying is really Jesus' response to Martha's expression in v. 24 that she would greet her brother again in a future resurrection. She was a believer, and she understood and acknowledged that there would be an ultimate resurrection in which she would see her brother again. Jesus' response to her is more poignant than that. He wants her to know that she will not just meet her brother again in a future resurrection, but she will inherit a life that will continue in the presence of God throughout eternity.

These words actually presage the lyrics of Jesus in 14:6. He is the essence of Life and therefore possesses power over death. He introduces the idea of eternal life, and it is Martha's faith, as it is with the faith of all Christians, that empowers Jesus to offer a quality of life that cannot be experienced outside a life of faith.

The final act of this drama comprises the miracle itself, vv. 33-44. At no time prior to the crucifixion is Jesus' human quality more self-evident than during this event. Verse 33 notes that He was "angry in His Spirit, and deeply moved," a distinct indicator of His humanity. The Greek term translated "angry" is ἐμβριμάομαι (*embrimaomai*) which has, as its root, to snort. It referred to the sound of an angry horse and expressed a kind of practical indignation. The word developed to include a deep feeling that is expressed both inwardly by emotion and outwardly by vocalization or other physical demonstration.[53] This feeling is further heightened by the additional use of ἐτάραξεν (*etaraxen*), an aorist form of ταράσσω (*tarassō*) which means agitate or trouble. Jesus clearly was vexed in spirit and sympathetic to the circumstances in which Mary, Martha and their friends

---

53. This Greek word is also used in 11:38 as Jesus approached the tomb to raise Lazarus.

found themselves. He did not hide His feelings of sadness, did not conceal His troubled spirit, but He responded as any compassionate human would respond.

Only here[54] and in 12:27 do we find where the emotions of Jesus are recorded in the Gospel. Even as the Son of God, Jesus kept His feelings in check, rarely revealing His true sentiments. Here Jesus unmistakably expressed His distress in some outward, physical expression, both by voice and body movement. The Synoptics record two other times when Jesus expressed emotion. Both of these accounts describe the same event, the time when Jesus wept over the city of Jerusalem.[55]

Can you remember those times when you attended a horror movie, and the scene was slowly unfolding to reveal something sinister or scary? You did not know what to expect. Perhaps you closed your eyes and covered your ears so as not to be frightened. The mystery of not knowing was the key to the moviemaker's plan. Such, perhaps, was the case with Martha. She did not know what to expect, only that in death, after four days, decomposition would have been firmly established.

Notice in v. 41 that Jesus prays over the situation. Was it necessary for the Son of God, who has the power over life and death, sickness and health, to pray to the Father? No! Jesus' prayer undoubtedly refers to the words spoken by Martha and is offered to emphasize the thought that the mighty deed about which He was to perform was a revelation of the glory of God. It was to be wrought in the name of the Father who had sent Jesus. So while Jesus did not need to ask for divine power, He actually uttered His prayer so that all might hear and know that the miracle to be accomplished was by no power of His own but by the

---

54. The "here" reference is to both v. 33 and v. 38.
55. Matthew 23:37 and Luke 19:41.

action of God through Him. Both His spoken prayer and His attitude are intended to make it plain that His power is derived solely from God.

Jesus calls to Lazarus, a form of the name Eleazar, which means "God helped." And Lazarus emerged from the tomb bound hand and foot. History describes such a dead body as having a cloth covering his face, wrappings or bindings wound tightly around his body from head to feet. Such a condition would have made it difficult to walk out of a tomb. Perhaps he stood and after standing, someone could have helped him out. Hoskyns concludes that Lazarus was "drawn out" of the tomb because his bindings would have prevented him from walking.[56] Perhaps so, but the focus is not on how he emerged but the fact *that* he emerged alive and well.

So Jesus meets the challenge of death. Death remains the primary problem of human existence and the ultimate issue for the individual. Death hangs like a Damocles sword over the world, but Jesus has the power to dispel any fear of death, the power to transcend our simple, human notions and the power to introduce the miraculous even in the twenty-first century.

What a marvelous story! Told by a dramatist whose crafty scripting of the event is unparalleled, this "sign" scored a significant impact on those who witnessed it. Even today it underscores the significance of the miraculous, spiritual power of Christ to those whose eyes behold His glory and acknowledge Him as the resurrection and the life.

---

56. Hoskyns, *op. cit.*, 407. This would have been reminiscent of 20:19 when the resurrected Jesus suddenly appeared to the disciples after the door had been shut and they were alone.

Chapter Six
John 11:47 – 14:26

Christ Rejected and Judgment on Israel, 11:47-12:50

C hrist, the Great Giver of Life, as illustrated in the raising of Lazarus from the dead, is regarded by the Gospeler as the supreme act that ultimately determined the fate of Jesus. On the one hand many of the Jews who either heard Jesus directly or heard about Him were moved to belief in Christ; on the other hand skeptics and conformist Jews who did not believe decided to report to the Pharisees, who persuaded the chief priests to call a meeting of the Sanhedrin. Whatever the Pharisees thought about the report, they recognized that the people at large were greatly impressed, and the increasing reputation of Jesus as a miracle worker was in danger of inciting a kind of messianic crusade which would attract the attention of the Roman authorities. Jesus did not hope for such a crusade, the disciples did not wish to get into the middle of a populace uprising of messianic hopes, but it was probably inevitable.

The Jews had been allotted limited freedom but considerable latitude under the rule of Rome, but times were changing and the current state of popular affairs was one of smoldering revolutionary feeling, which culminated in the rebellion of AD 66 and the ultimate destruction of the Temple in AD 70. Their fear of the repercussions from Jesus' popularity is reflected in their concern for loss of their "place" and "nation" in v. 48. The word translated "place" is τόπον (*topon*), the accusative form of τόπος (*topos*). It has variously been interpreted to refer to the Sanhedrin, the unique, identifiable body of Judaism; it could refer to the land which the Jews had inherited and in which they dwelt; or it could have referred to the Temple, the focal point of Judaism. It seems appropriate to dismiss the idea of the land, because the Jews could, once again, have been forced into slavery and evicted from the land and moved to a limited geographical area not unlike their time in Egypt or Babylon. Since the Sanhedrin was more interested in power and authority over the Jews than being good Romans, and since it was unique to the Jews and so peculiar to Judaism, the members probably deferred to their Supreme Council, the Sanhedrin. They reasoned that if they lost their "place," they lost the ability to rule over their people, the Jews, religiously.

"Nation," ἔθνος (*ethnos*), defines a race, people or nation and refers specifically, singularly, to the nation of Israel. By employing this term the Sanhedrin implied that the Jews might even vanish as a people if Jesus were to be permitted to continue unrestrained. By losing the "nation," they inferred that they would lose not only the Sanhedrin, one of the distinguishing marks of Judaism but also their identity as a people. The idea of losing "place" and "nation" became sufficiently serious potential consequences as to cause the Sanhedrin to initiate a capture of Jesus.

After hearing all the evidence and the potential damaging results that might occur if Jesus were allowed to persist in His ministry, Caiaphas, the High Priest, decided that steps should be taken immediately to silence Jesus once and for all. His decision was a cold-blooded and deliberate incitement to murder, but it carried the day. From that moment, Jesus was doomed.

In making the announcement of his decision in vv. 50-52, Caiaphas fulfilled his calling as a prophet. In ancient times prophetic foretelling was considered to be a gift of the priesthood. The motive of Caiaphas in making his statement in v. 50 was only to seize Jesus and put Him to death. In reality, he utters a prophecy, the real meaning of which completely escapes him. But the prophecy was in keeping with God's purpose of salvation for the whole world. And even as these sentiments were being expressed by Caiaphas, Jesus withdrew with His disciples to Ephraim, some 14 miles north of Jerusalem, essentially foiling the immediate plans of the Sanhedrin because the "hour" hand of the Father's clock had not yet struck the appointed time.

While this section, including the rejection of Christ, has been designated as beginning in chapter 11, it more accurately begins for the Gospeler in chapter 12. The passage describing the rejection of Jesus and the pronouncement of judgment upon Israel is comprised of two distinct happenings throughout this chapter. These happenings begin with the anointing of Jesus, vv. 1-11. Other descriptions of an account of Jesus' anointing occur in all three Synoptic Gospels—Matthew (26:6-13), Mark (14:3-9) and Luke (7:36-39). Why these accounts differ so markedly is not known. However, it is believed by many scholars that the narratives may, in fact, depict the same occurrence and that John decided to take certain liberties with the facts to remain focused upon and to achieve his purpose.

The Anointing of Jesus, 12:1-11

The anointing of Jesus took place at Bethany. The Synoptics locate the anointing at the home of Simon.[57] John places it at the home of Mary, Martha and Lazarus. In the Matthean account, the timing of the event is two days prior to the Passover. In John's Gospel, however, the time is set six days prior to the final Passover, or Nisan 8. Arriving a bit after sunset, Jesus would have shared a Sabbath meal with the group. Although the Synoptic accounts do not include the name of the anointing woman, John identifies her as Mary of Bethany, most probably the sister of Martha and Lazarus.

Mary produces a jar or bottle of nard[58] or quite expensive ointment and anoints Jesus' feet while He was reclining at dinner. While there appears to be some editing from tradition in this story,[59] the truth of the story yet remains symbolic and true—namely that Mary is, in actuality, anointing the living body of Jesus, a body that will soon lie in death inside a borrowed garden tomb. The words of v. 7, "she has kept it for the day of my burial" indicates that Mary did not consume all of the ointment when she anointed Jesus' feet, but some of the ointment remained in the container, and, though not acknowledged by her, that amount was to be devoted to the preparation of the deceased body of Jesus for burial.

One final word is essential to complete the thought of these verses. Judas takes umbrage with the "waste" of the

---

57. Matthew 26:6f; Mark 14:3f; Luke 7:36f.

58. Nard is a short form of "spikenard," a plant found in the Himalayas used to produce a fragrant ointment or perfume. Mary used the ointment form of this quite expensive balm.

59. Matthew and Mark write that the ointment was applied to the head of Jesus. Luke's account has the woman's tears anointing the feet of Jesus.

ointment by Mary. The ointment was very expensive for the day, and he wished it to be sold and used for the poor. Was he really interested in helping the poor? No, he was simply a common thief who had often pilfered the treasury of the disciples. He had stolen from other people, he had stolen from those closest to him and was not at all interested in helping the poor. So not only, then, does John imply by act of anointment the demise of Jesus, but he also deliberately juxtaposes the generosity of Mary against the mercenary intent of Judas. What a contrast!

Seventh Manifestation: The Triumphal Entry into Jerusalem, 12:12-19

John includes the second "happening" in this final thrust toward Calvary as yet another manifestation of the nature of Jesus. In v. 12-19, he describes the triumphal entry of Jesus into Jerusalem, which actually initiates the passion narrative. This act of homage, which proclaimed Jesus as the Messiah, is yet another way in which the Gospeler offers a dramatic glimpse of the crushing evil that permeated the souls of the Jewish leaders who were determined to bring an end to this trouble-maker. Not only were they out to terminate Jesus, but they resolved to destroy anyone with whom He might have been associated, especially with respect to His miracles. Lazarus, and the miracle of his resurrection, fit that bill.

The entire event comprises a messianic demonstration on the part of the people and Jesus. Its meaning for the Gospeler is far deeper than the simple outward journey through the streets of Jerusalem.

First, we read of the "palm branches" that were strewn along the path upon which Jesus rode. Palms were common to the area in ancient times and were readily available. Palm branches were representative of royal victory, of the joy experienced by conquerors after a war. But for John they represent the victory of one who is, even in life, already a conqueror over death. This procession represents the "regal advent of the Messiah . . . in peace and in humility."[60]

The crowd cries out, "Hosanna," translated as "save us we pray." Drawn from Psalm 118:26, the cry of the crowd echoes John's view of and faith in the person of Jesus. This King of Israel is He who comes now, experiences the agony of death and who, after returning to the Father for a time, will come again for His saints who have remained faithful. He *is* the Messiah of John.

Note in v. 14 the manner of His entry. He comes riding upon a donkey. While the most apparent interpretation of this act would be to illustrate Jesus' humility, such is likely not the case. The animal is a messianic symbol, but it is also an image of Him entering a city where He will reign as king and Messiah.[61] The animal represented the fulfillment of the prophecy of Zechariah. Jesus, familiar with this prophecy,[62] deliberately chose this means of presenting Himself. John intentionally connects Jesus' appearance on the donkey with the words of Zechariah in order to underscore the fulfillment of yet another Old Testament prophecy. While the populace, who scattered the palm branches before Jesus did not recognize the import of their actions, His entry into Jerusalem, in fact, represents Jesus' official presentation as the Messiah. He had revealed Himself as the Messiah through six "signs," now He manifests Himself symbolically as Messiah from prophecy. He is the Suffering

60. *Ibid.*, 420.
61. See Revelation 3:12 and 21:2.
62. Zechariah 9:9-10.

Servant of Isaiah who comes on an errand of peace, not as a great conquering hero.

Pericope, The Coming of the Greeks, 12:19-36

In the midst of the tumult of the hour, John chooses to include yet another pericope. The appearance of the Greeks, as short-lived as it is, serves a valuable purpose—to confirm that the mission of Jesus, once complete, will be for all people, Jews and Gentiles alike. These persons who sought to see Jesus were not Jews but were more likely Greek proselytes to Judaism who adhered to the moral teachings of the faith and the worship of one God. Though they were Jews by choice, and they elected to worship at the Temple, Josephus writes that they were, nevertheless, restricted to the outer court of the Gentiles.[63] Their presence in this account foretells the universal nature of the gospel and the world-wide mission of the greater church that would follow.

Whether these Greeks actually met Jesus is unknown, but the occasion gave Jesus the opportunity to clarify His purpose on earth. At this point in His ministry, He was aware that the "hour" for the fulfillment of the mission to which the Father had called Him was fast approaching.

In order to illustrate His point graphically, Jesus employs an agricultural metaphor which His listeners would most certainly comprehend. Practical in nature, Jesus notes that life in the plant kingdom does not regenerate until a seed falls into the ground and dies. In the same way, vital to providing eternal life will be His own faithfulness to the plan set forth by the Father from the beginning, namely, that He die so that He might bring "life" to all. A different kind of life, but life nevertheless. He was acutely aware of

---

63. Josephus, *Bellum Judaicum*, VI, 422-426.

what lay ahead, yet He would be obedient to the Father in spite of the horror that He knew He would endure.

The divinely appointed time is at hand; the earthly ministry of Jesus is about to come to its conclusion. Jesus must be resolute, and His determination to do the will of the Father will excise an excruciating cost. The words of v. 27 remind us a bit of Gethsemane and Jesus' inner desire to avoid the Cross. While not recorded in the Gospel of John, all three Synoptic Gospels[64] record the words of Jesus in the Garden that night. Nowhere is His humanity more evident than in His prayer that the "cup" be removed. Although as much human as He was divine and as much divine as He was human, John portrays Jesus as one whose longing to be obedient to the Father overshadows His human emotion.

God the Father acknowledges Jesus' ultimate glorification by speaking, "I have glorified it, and I will glorify it again," v. 28. Was this voice audible to the crowd? Both Jesus' response and John's depiction would beg belief that they heard something. Some said it sounded like thunder; others, to whom words may have been clearly understood, heard the voice of an angel.

The soul—or life—of Jesus was deeply troubled, not because of the dreadful, lonely ordeal that He confronted but by the pain of knowing what His disciples might endure both in the present and in the future. As a man, He was torn with passion and sadness. Nevertheless, as God, He was aware that, to be obedient to the Father, the hour for His glorification was at hand. Nowhere is that more evident than in v. 32.

Unfamiliar utterings by Jesus? Hardly. They had heard Him speak on this subject in 3:14; He is now applying the principle specifically to Himself. Did the Jews grasp that Jesus referred to His death? Perhaps they did as evidenced

---

64. Matthew 26:39, Mark 14:36, and Luke 22:42.

in v. 34. Their disappointment is unmistakable, however, as witnessed by their words, "We have heard from the scripture that the Messiah will remain forever." They believed that once the Messiah came, He would remain among them, certainly not be put to death. Derisive words, indeed. In truth, the Chosen People of God had ignored the claims of Christ, holding fast to the idea that the true Messiah would be a deliverer, his death was not part of the tradition.

The public ministry of Jesus is about to come to its conclusion. From this point forward, John describes the closing stage of the intimate relationship with the disciples before the last tragic scenes of the betrayal, trial and crucifixion. His interaction ceases with the public and continues solely with the disciples and the Roman government from this point forward. His ministry among the Jews ceases to be. By being "lifted up," He will no longer be a Messiah for the Jews only but will become the universal Saviour for all mankind, regardless of race.

Light still penetrates the darkest of corners, and the Light of God's salvation shined upon some of the Jewish rulers. But cowards they turned out to be. While quietly believing in Jesus as the Christ, they refused to confess Him because they cared more for their social standing and cultural acceptance than their relationship with God, v. 42-43. Their eyes were blinded and their hearts hardened.

This chapter closes with a summary of the public ministry of Jesus. The words of vv. 44-50 reflect both who Jesus is and the content and source of His teachings. In v. 44 Jesus is represented as an ambassador for the Father. He so symbolizes the One who sent Him that belief in one is belief in the other, for the ambassador possesses no authority except that granted by the sovereign whom he represents. The assertion of v. 50 summarizes this concept. Jesus' words are His Father's words, and belief in those words ushers in salvation.

The Beginning of the End, 13:1-30

Notable from the beginning of chapter 13 is the absence of any preparatory efforts for the Last Supper on the part of Jesus' disciples as written in the Synoptics. John, being mindful of the Markan account of the Supper, envisaged no necessity to include details which were already identified and established. Such details would add no profundity or spiritual significance to his objective. His aim was far more theological and spiritual.

The timing of the Supper is of particular importance. Passover would have occurred beginning on Thursday evening (at sunset) and would have continued until Friday at sunset.[65] By such a reckoning, Jesus' death, which followed on Friday, Nisan 14, would correspond with the sacrifice of the paschal lamb.

Eighth Manifestation: The Upper Room Cleansing, 13:5-12

Both Jesus' words and actions during the cleansing ceremony, the eighth manifestation of Jesus' nature, declare a special message. His disciples, who represented the New Israel, must be purged of dependence upon the Law and the Prophets for deliverance, and only He could effect such a cleansing. The ultimate cleansing would be seen in His sacrifice on the Cross. After this final cleansing, a new commandment of love is offered and eventually, the Second Paraclete.

---

65. The Jews determined the day as beginning at sunset and ending at sunset. Therefore, the words of 13:1 would imply that the Supper was held before sunset on Thursday, Nisan 13.

The washing of the disciples' feet is an "acted parable" in which Jesus uses actions instead of words to convey a truth. It is a spiritual symbol with a spiritual message. One interpretation is that Jesus was illustrating humility by employing such a servile act. But He was not so much demonstrating humility as He was the act of cleansing. This act described by John is purely theological and spiritual. It has little to do with physicality.

The act, in which Jesus is about to engage, was a common occurrence of ancient times when house servants would wash the feet of dinner guests as they arrived. Its purpose was to remove the dust or dirt from their feet which they collected from the dusty streets of the city. We know from the Synoptics that the conversation in the room included a discussion of who would be greatest in the kingdom to come. From such a conversation one would naturally conclude that the purpose of this act was to exemplify humility. Jesus puts that colloquy to rest.

At this point, He is dressed as and represents the quintessential Teacher of Israel. He set aside those garments in favor of an apron, a kind of towel, and assumed the role of a servant. Likely beginning with Peter, He washed the disciples' feet, drying them with another towel, not the one around His waist.

This story of the feet washing ceremony is a symbol of the voluntary indignity of Jesus and foreshadows the indignity that He will endure over the next few days. However, it is much more than that. Its true significance would be revealed only after His death on the Cross, and it would be then that the disciples would finally grasp a complete awareness of the true meaning of discipleship.

Note once again that the disciples represent the New Israel, Jesus represents the Teacher of Israel cleansing the Old Israel and through His death on the Cross will ultimately bring cleansing to them. But one must be willing to put on a servant's garment, be willing to become a servant to one another to personify the cleansing power of the death of Christ. It was at this crucial and incisive moment that the Eleven acknowledged the power represented in them, the New Israel, the κοινωνία (koinōnia),[66] that ultimately developed into the church of Jesus Christ. The disciples were now the New Israel, and all Christians are their descendants, the inheritors of the New Israel. All believers have been liberated from the Law just as were the early disciples.

If Jesus conceded the need for cleansing and willingly participated in an act of such humility to exemplify it, why does the act of foot washing not serve as a sacrament or ordinance in today's church? Ordinances and sacraments (terminology used by several traditions) are so designated because they offer symbols that are related to the death, burial and resurrection of Jesus. The washing of the disciples' feet tenders no such import, possesses no such meaning. It is an act of cleansing only; humility is secondary to the act.

What follows is a proclamation or foretelling of the soon betrayal of Jesus. What has been insinuated in v. 11 now gives way to a definitive prediction. John offers no names so the act of disclosing the betrayer was an enigma to the disciples. Between v. 11 and v. 27 there was a final appeal to Judas to refrain from his diabolical intent, his devilish desire, and the action of Jesus (v. 26b) was, in John's view, one of kindness.[67] Jesus concerned Himself with Judas' spirituality and wished for him to be a genuine part of the

---

66. Though Jesus also washed the feet of Judas, the outward cleansing had no purposeful effect upon his heart and soul.

67. Jesus handed a "morsel" of bread to Judas just as he had done with the other disciples.

disciple band. In v. 27 John clearly acknowledges (perhaps even after the Supper) that the inevitable treachery of betrayal was final.

So Judas departs! This man, who was probably not legitimate even while he was a disciple, was a prevaricator, and he certainly gave Jesus up quite easily.

However, it is not out of hatred or disdain for his spiritual mentor that he leaves, rather it is the lust of greed and the power of love in the person of Jesus that expelled Judas from the band of disciples so gathered. And so it is with the true church of Jesus Christ—the Judases can never remain because the power of Christ's love is overwhelming and irresistible. If a church is not doing the will of the Father, unwilling to accept and share the love of Jesus, it is, as Judas was, forever relegated to the realm of darkness.

The Initial Farewell Discourse of Jesus, 13:31-14:31

These words of Jesus comprise one of His farewell discourses which shapes the final message He wishes to utter to His disciples. They are the declaration of a great Christian Prophet presiding at the Lord's Table. The "hour" about which He has spoken so often has now arrived and His glorification awaits. The "hour," to be inaugurated by an act of treachery is, in reality, the moment when God's redemptive activity reaches its climax.

As Jesus addressed His disciples in v. 33, the warmth of His words was revealed in the salutation, τεκνία (*teknia*), "children." One of Paul's favorite terms, it was often used by rabbis when addressing their students. Jesus regards His disciples as "learners" who will continue to develop spiritually and become declarers of the kind of love that He has both taught and exemplified. Their love, the love of the disciples, the love of the New Israel, the love of the church

111

will be characterized by a new and different quality. It will become the mark of true discipleship, and it will embrace a "new commandment" under a new covenant. Jesus speaks this "commandment" in vv. 34-35.

The prescience of Jesus is keenly illustrated in His prediction of Peter's actions during Jesus' forthcoming ordeal. He tells Peter that, in spite of his faithfulness and his declarations of loyalty, he will deny Jesus three times before the crucifixion. Does the number three convey any hidden meaning in the message of the crucifixion? All of the Synoptics refer to a triple denial of Jesus by Peter leading the reader to conclude that the number probably has little real substance in the last days narrative. However, the Gospeler may have concluded otherwise.

In Hebrew numerology the number three represents holiness, completeness, stability. Jesus had earlier designated Simon as "Peter" in acknowledgment of his rock solid nature, his strength and dedication as a follower. Peter would have done anything to support and protect his Master. Later, in the Garden of Gethsemane, he will put himself in harms way before a garrison of Roman soldiers to protect Jesus. That is who Peter was!

Now that rock solid nature and dedication would be put to the test. At this moment, Peter's heart and mind were focused on the impending betrayal, separation and death of Jesus. He had suspicions regarding what might happen to him shortly, especially since the Jews had been pursuing Him for quite some time and particularly since the raising of Lazarus. But he cannot imagine abandoning his Master. Nevertheless, his holiness and stability will be challenged over the next few days, and Jesus declares that he will fail the test. But his failure would be the catalyst to complete in him a holy quality unequalled among the disciple band, a faithfulness of everlasting proportions and a stability in love for Jesus that led to his ultimate martyrdom. In the pressures of modern society, how often do we, like Peter, fail the test? As strong and as impenetrable by evil as we think we might be, beset by the spears and arrows of the world, how well do we perform when the time of testing comes? If Peter can fail, so can we! But just as Peter did, we can come through the valley of failure to a mountain peak of holiness and completeness.

The Messages of the Upper Room, 14:1-31

Jesus knows that His disciples have been troubled by the prediction of His betrayal and death. They do not comprehend all that He has said, but they are disturbed by what they do understand. Jesus, too, is aware that the shock of these events will be troubling to them, especially once they occur. The disciples, as well as the Jews as a people, were seeking a military Messiah, a Christ of kingly proportions who would come in military fashion and would rule the world. The Messiah that they are observing is simply not the kind of Messiah that they expected.

Jesus now announces His intention to "go away." Do the disciples understand what He means by "go away"? Probably not, and certainly not completely. Yet He tries to make it clear in 14:1f. He feels compelled to offer His disciples a sense of solace in an attempt to assuage their despair because they are aware that the Jews are determined to seize Jesus and charge Him with treason. So His words are intended to put their minds at peace. Once more He pronounces His oneness with the Father, a statement that is reminiscent of earlier declarations, v. 1.

The "many dwelling places" of v. 2 translates μοναὶ πολλαί (*monai pollai*) which can also refer to rooms, resting places or abiding places. Jesus tells His disciples that all who believe in Him as the Son of God will find a place of rest in the Father's house. There is room for all; no one who believes in Him will be rejected. To the disciples this is a good word, a happy word. What a consolation to the weary, earth-bound traveler whose life has been beset with travail, pain and uncertainty. Jesus goes to a place prepared by His Father for all who will rest in Jesus from their terrestrial journey. What an assurance that none of God's children is forgotten, but they find rest in the presence of the Eternal Father, the only One that really matters.

John closes this section of this narrative in v. 6 with another of the "I AM" statements of Jesus. Appropriate to this line of thought, Jesus says, "I am THE way, and THE truth, and THE life." With respect to this saying, Robertson wrote, "He is the Incarnation of God, the Personification of truth, and the Energy of life."[68]

In the Greek text each of the elements of this phrase includes the definite article. By attaching the definite article to the noun, John specifies Jesus as the "only" one of each of these characteristics. As ἡ ὁδός (hē hodos), Jesus is "the way," the sole pathway to eternal rest and the brilliant presence of the Father and the Son. Only by trusting through faith in His atoning death can "the way" be paved for the ultimate renewal of the soul into a spiritual body that will abide in a "resting place" forever. Jesus is not simply a director of traffic to a heavenly abode, He is the road, the way to that heavenly abode.[69]

He is also ἡ ἀλήθεια (hē alētheia), "the truth." As "the truth" He is the sole revelation of the One True God. He is divine reality; He is ultimate truth because He is one with and has been sent by the Giver of all truth. Without Him self-realization is impossible because one cannot know

---

68. Robertson, *op. cit.,* 117.
69. Note the early designation of Christians as "The Way."

oneself apart from knowing God. To know Jesus is to know all truth, not all facts, but all truth.

Truth is that upon which we base our lives. What if we could not trust truth? Life would not be as we know it; life would simply be like a vision. Nothing around us would be real; but life is real because God is real, and God is real because Jesus is real, and the two are One. So Jesus is the truth.

Finally He is ἡ ζωή (hē zōē), "the life." As the embodiment of ultimate truth, Jesus is the "way" that leads to eternal "life," real life in its ultimate state. John has employed this term thirty-one times in his Gospel to this point, so it is important to him that Jesus' words resonate with the idea of "life" as the concluding element of a phrase that summarizes the divine nature of Jesus and His ultimate gift through His ministry and sacrifice. Hoskyns says He is "both the Truth and the Life. He gives the Life which He is, He reveals the Truth which He is, He offers the Life which He is, just as He speaks the Word and provides the Bread which He is. Consequently He is the Way, as He is the Door. No man can attain the Father except by perceiving the Truth and participating in the Life which is revealed to men in His Son."[70]

The Paraclete, 14:16-26

These verses represent one of John's two discourses on the Paraclete interrupted by more words of assurance for His disciples. Both Paraclete treatments employ the term παράκλητος (paraklētos) which is variously translated as "Helper" (NASV), "Counselor" (RSV), or "Comforter" (KJV). Its literal meaning is "one called alongside" and refers generally to any kind of helper or advocate.

---

70. Hoskyns, op. cit., 455.

The Johannine meaning of παράκλητος (*paraklētos*) is more comprehensive in that John incorporates both a revelatory and eschatological nuance to the term. Revelatory in that the idea of a Paraclete reveals something about Jesus. It reveals something about God in John. But it also possesses an eschatological nuance to it, because Jesus says that He will go away and will "come back," v. 3.

Notice that Jesus says that the Father will send "another Helper." Who then is the first Helper? It is none other than Jesus Himself. Acknowledging that the Paraclete is the revelation of God, Jesus, as a part of the Trinity, is the Holy Spirit, the First Paraclete, but He will soon depart this world and return to the Father making it necessary for the appearance of another Paraclete. This second Paraclete will abide forever and will be called the "Spirit of truth." But as "you will know the truth, and the truth will set you free," so shall the Spirit of truth inhabit the spirit and soul of those who acknowledge its presence and the Truth of the Son who declared it.

While not considered to be a pericope, vv. 18-24 comprise a brief return to the subject with which Jesus initiated this chapter, peace of mind. Jesus offers yet another note of consolation to His disciples and to believers of generations yet to be. He offers assurance that He will not leave them or us alone ("as orphans") but will dwell in the hearts and souls of those who keep His commandments. Outside the church, outside the body of believers, outside the family of God, no spiritual regeneration can exist. Jesus, therefore, offers them the satisfaction that they will never be alone as long as they are in a relationship with Him.

Then John returns for a second discourse on the Paraclete, vv. 26f. Here Jesus assures the disciples that the Holy Spirit, that is the Paraclete who will follow Him, will be dedicated to continuing the work of Jesus through

His followers. This Holy Spirit, a revelation of God sent by the Father in the name of Jesus, will reinforce the faith of believers through teachable moments and will keep the words of Jesus present in the minds and hearts of believers.

From the two Paraclete discourses, John offers several conclusions. First, Jesus was the first Holy Spirit, a revelation of God sent to die and through whose death salvation might be made available to all who accept Him. As a part of the Trinity, He is one with the Father, He possesses the inheritance of the Son and He is omnipresent as the Holy Spirit.

Second, the Holy Spirit, the Second Paraclete, is pure Spirit. The world could seize the first Spirit, and they could crucify Him, but they could neither destroy Him nor the Holy Spirit that followed (16:7).

Third, the Holy Spirit is, indeed, Paraclete, one who is called alongside to be our counselor, comforter, advocate. He is our constant companion in this earthly pilgrimage and enlightens our hearts and souls with spiritual encouragement from God the Father.

Fourth, the Holy Spirit is the spirit of truth, not the spirit of foolishness. The Holy Spirit is prudent, thoughtful, wise. There is no room for foolhardiness or folly.

Fifth, the Holy Spirit is representative of Jesus in the world (14:18, 26). The Holy Spirit never operates independent of Jesus (15:26f) but enjoys and reflects all of the characteristics of the Father and the Son.

Chapter Seven

John 15:1 – 17:26

Ninth Manifestation: The True Vine, 15:1-11

Only the incarnation makes possible a vital relationship between the people of God and God Himself. The historic Jesus revealed God to the realm of the real and actual, for it is in Him that we can see and know God in His fullness. Our awareness of God is as an ethereal kind of being, but when He came in Jesus Christ, He came to the world of the tangible, the real.

Our consciousness of God is retained by a relationship with Christ through the Holy Spirit. Authentic faith, i. e., true religion, is an "I-Thou" relationship with Christ but not apart from the true church.

John describes the ninth manifestation, a continuation of the series of farewell discourses, by introducing the final of the seven "I AM" saying of Jesus. "I am the true vine." The setting continues to be in the Upper Room at the Last Supper, where Jesus washed the feet of the disciples and conversed with them about both his immediate and his long-range future. Truly this gathering was a rather protracted event. Now He wishes to enlighten them a bit about their future. Jesus has already discussed His future, now He will discuss theirs.

Jesus turns to the allegory of the vine so often associated with Israel in the Old Testament. One of the most recognized symbols of the Jewish faith, the menorah, has its origins in the symbol of the vine.[71] Even during the time of the Maccabees, the vine symbol adorned the coins. Here Jesus employs this same symbol for the Messiah, His church and His followers. It is truly a picture of the Messiah as the ideal Israelite with the remnant of Israel, the disciples.

In these verses, three phrases capture the major ideas of this discourse. In v. 1, Jesus says, "I am the true vine." We know from experience that the vine is the medium of life; it is the conduit of vitality and sustenance from the root to the branches to the leaves. Since Jesus is the vine, He thus is the One who supplies life-giving nourishment to the branches; He is the medium through which we understand life by His teachings of great ethical principles. He is the One who nurtures life by His example, by being the representative man. He is the One who nurtures life by His death which empowers us for victory over sin. He is the One who nurtures life by His resurrection—through the continuing, living presence of the Holy Spirit.

The second major idea also occurs in v. 1 where Jesus says, "My Father is the vineyard keeper." This would have been a common and familiar picture to the disciples. Because they lived in an agricultural environment, the disciples, and hence, the populace at large, would have understood the meaning of His word pictures. So He often

---

71. See Psalm 80:8-9.

spoke in parables. The discourse offered here in the Upper Room could be classified as a parable as well.

Jesus declares that His Father is the keeper and the preserver of the vineyard. So, I, as a member of the true church, am under the watchful supervision and attention of His preserving, loving, tender and compassionate care. Nothing is out of the sphere of the Father's will, and when necessary, He prunes the fruit from the branches or prunes the branches themselves.

Interpreting the "pruning" has sometimes presented a challenge. Three possible interpretations seem fitting with respect to the action, or perhaps the pruning might be any one of these interpretations occurring at different stages of life. These interpretations include, first, the continuous cleansing of sin by confession or contrition.

The picture Jesus is painting is that of the church and the life-sustaining relationship between Him and His followers. The branches that do not bear fruit represent (1) unbelievers, (2) apostate Israel and even (3) unrepentant Judas. But still those branches that do bear fruit occasionally must be pruned as in the case of Peter whose denial represented a moment of fruitlessness. As in the agricultural world where plants are pruned so that they may be renewed and increase production, so Christians may be pruned so that they may produce more and better fruit. So it was with Peter. He was pruned so that he might bear more fruit.

Does God cause suffering because we sin? Be careful how we answer that question! God does not sit on His throne waiting for us to sin and then "zaps" us for sinning. We do not worship that kind of a God. Remember, however, we are made in the "image of God." One key manner in which we are made in the "image of God" is our volition, free will. If, in my free will, I decide to act in a way that violates

God's laws of physics, I will suffer. God is not generally in the business of suspending the laws of physics to save a life, although miracles do still occur. Logically then, John declares that, if you are willing to use your free will against the will of God, to act stubbornly against the will of God, you will suffer life's natural consequences.

A second interpretation of pruning is the closing of doors to the realization of selfish desires and egotistical ambitions. During those times when our desires, whether materially or spiritually, good or not good, are inconsistent with the will of God, then pruning can be expected. It is important that all of our requests, made known to God, are expressed ultimately by "Thy will be done." If it was good enough for Jesus who said "Now my soul is troubled. What shall I say—'Father, save Me from this hour?' But that is why I came to this hour" (John 12:27), it is good enough for us. If it was good enough for Jesus who suffered bloody, sweat-stained agony in the Garden of Gethsemane yet cried, "Not my will, but Yours, be done" (Luke 22:42, 44), it is good enough for us. If it was good enough for Jesus who pled with the Father to "Let this cup pass from Me. Yet not as I will, but as you will" (Matthew 26:39), it is good enough for us.

A third interpretation might be through suffering, when God compels me to accept life's tragedy, to rise above it and to use it for His glory. Jesus is the supreme example of this interpretation. Jesus was not being pruned, but certainly He rose above the suffering, and He was glorified as a result. Unexpected events may occur to us at times with no real explanation. Perhaps wrong place, wrong time. Perhaps even the result of someone else not in the will of God that spills over onto us. But God will ask in the process of pruning us to use that experience for His glory not our own.

Recall the story of Job. The influence of Satan in our lives cannot be discounted. The power of Satan can influence our lives unimaginably, causing us to perform acts or commit sins never dreamed. And we may suffer the pruning process as a result of submitting to the temptations of the Evil One. He will tempt us in inconceivable ways, and he possesses the power to bring onto us sufferings that we are urged by the Father to defeat.

Whatever form the pruning might take, the strength, conviction and faithfulness of the believer will be tested. God's desire for those who are tested is that the authenticity of their relationship with God will be evidenced through their successful traverse through the struggle.[72]

The experience of pruning is not one to be enjoyed, and it may be at those times perhaps that we may feel that God has abandoned us. We may be suffering or feel disillusioned or walking through the shadows. These times of pruning are the times when God can mold us and make us into what He wills us to be.

At times, God, the Father, the vinedresser, separates a dead branch from the vine. If a branch does not bear fruit, then it is considered to be a dead branch and is not worthy of the name Christian. But such judgment is God's to make not ours; God alone possesses the right to judge and to remove.

The final major idea of the vine metaphor appears in v. 5 where Jesus said, "You are the branches." Here John is stating that a vital union with the vine is maintained by abiding and living in Christ, by the presence of His living words in us. In so doing, we are to be submissive to Christ's teachings. As obedient children then, we, the branches, prove by our fruit-bearing, the life-receiving interconnection with the vine.

72. Paul reminds us of this principle in 1 Corinthians 10:13.

What are the fruits about which John speaks? The text does not address the exact meaning of the fruit, but it surely must include love, a holy life, communion with God in prayer, a ministry of evangelism and stewardship of life.[73] Therefore, if we are in the world and not bearing these kinds of fruit, we may be subject to pruning by the will of God.

In vv. 4-7 John encapsulates the message of the entire passage. The branch is one not only with the vine, but it is also one with the other branches. One branch cannot bear fruit of itself, and so John accentuates the oneness of the body of Christ.[74] The church should never be neglected or de-emphasized as the body of Christ but should remain firmly connected to the vine through spiritual maturity and fruit bearing.

A wonderful illustration of this oneness with the vine is that of the testimony of retired Air Force Colonel Buzz Aldrin, the second man to walk on the moon.

> *One day while I was at Cape Kennedy working with the sophisticated tools of the space effort, it occurred to me that these tools were the typical elements of life today. I wondered if it might be possible to take communion on the moon, symbolizing the thought that God was revealing Himself there too, as man reached out into the universe. For there are many of us in the NASA program who do trust that what we are doing is part of God's eternal plan for man. I spoke with [Pastor Dean Woodruff] about the idea as soon as I returned home, and*

---

73. Compare these to the fruits of the Spirit in Galatians 5:22-23. Are they parallel? Do they mean the same?

74. Could Paul have been thinking about these words when he wrote in Romans 12:4-5?

he was enthusiastic. "I could carry the bread in a plastic packet, the way regular inflight food is wrapped. And the wine also—there will be just enough gravity on the moon for liquid to pour. I'll be able to drink normally from a cup. Dean, I wonder if you could look around for a little chalice that I could take with me as coming from the church?" The next week Dean showed me a graceful silver cup. I hefted it and was please to find that it was light enough to take along. Each astronaut is allowed a few personal items on a flight; the wine chalice would be in my personal preference kit. Then while on the moon's surface, Aldrin finally took communion after the 240,000 mile journey. Now Neil and I were sitting inside Eagle, while Mike (Collins) circled in lunar orbit unseen in the black sky above us. In a little while after our scheduled meal period, Neil would give the signal to step down the ladder onto the powdery surface of the moon. Now was the moment for communion. So I unstowed the elements in their flight packets. I put them and the scripture reading on the little table in front of the abort guidance system computer. Then I called back to Houston. "Houston, this is Eagle. This is the LM pilot speaking. I would like to request a few moments of silence. I would like to invite each person listening in, wherever and whomever he may be, to contemplate for a moment the events of the past few hours and to give thanks in his own individual way." I poured the wine into the chalice our church had given me. In the one-sixth gravity of the moon the wine curled slowly and gracefully up the side of the cup. It was interesting to think that the very first liquid ever poured on the moon, and the first food eaten there, were communion elements. And so, just before I partook of the elements, I read the words which I had chosen to indicate our trust that as man probes into space we are in fact acting in Christ. I sensed especially strongly my unity with our church back home, and with the Church everywhere. I read: "I am the vine, you are the branches. Whoever remains in me, and I in him, will bear much fruit; for you can do nothing without me."[75]

What a wonderful reminder that the picture of the vine and the branches is one of unity—unity with God, unity in the church and unity with one another. Vine and branches abiding with each other, and branches and branches abiding together, make for a church impervious to the temptations of the world to be less than what we are called to be.

John describes a fruitful branch as a believer who has the privilege of asking and receiving the Father's good gifts, v. 7. But a true believer does not ask selfishly. Self-regarding entreaties would not be viewed by God, I believe, as being in the best interest of His Kingdom.

Rather, "thy will be done" is the believer's guiding principle. Specific requests should also be consistent with the Father's will. We often get confused by the use of this phrase because Christians are tempted to use it as an excuse. For example, when we pray for a friend to live who is obviously dying, we may pray, "Lord, heal this person." But we fail to add the caveat, "Your will be done." Sometimes it is not God's will for that person to live. God

75. Buzz Aldrin, "Communion in Space," *Guideposts*, October 1970.

sees the past, present and future; we know the past and present, but we do not know the future. Through that friend's death a greater good, of which God is aware, may result. Any prayer, plea or petition to God should include the "will of the Father." Thus the believer partakes of the good gifts in Jesus Christ when he is in contact with the source of all life and submissive to that source.

New Relationships, 15:12-27

Jesus declared, beginning in v. 12, that the fundamental characteristic of this new community to be called the church will be "love." This love is unequivocal, unselfish and unconditional and is sufficient to transform them from slave to friend, a condition exemplified by the Master's love for them. These slaves and their masters are changed by the Gospel. While they may still be master and slave in their physical relationship, their spiritual relationship in the church changes.

Jesus now sends the disciples on mission into a hateful and hostile world that will not always respond affirmatively to the self-sacrificing love they are called to exhibit. Their message will be a witness of their own experiences with Jesus, but sometimes they can expect the world to treat them even as the world treated Jesus.

The disciples are to love each other, v. 12, and to remain diligent in the mission to which they are being sent. Because He is love, Jesus has the right to command this same love of His disciples. Such love for each other will be necessary as they confront the hatred of the world. They have been somewhat insulated at this point. Jesus has protected them, but they will not be protected once He is gone.

Jesus urged them to understand that the world's hatred, which they will subsequently encounter, was first experienced by Him, vv. 18-25. In v. 25 He quotes Psalm 35:19 from the Law as a prophecy of the antagonism that He so often faced.

Their love for each other will grant the kind of moral support needed to fuel their ministry and supply encouragement in the face of opposition. They will possess one advantage, however, that was not available to Jesus, the Holy Spirit, v. 26. The witness of the Paraclete, this Holy Spirit, will ultimately prove effective in their mission because both they and the Spirit bear witness to the truth.

The Farewell Discourse Concludes, 16:1-33

There is little doubt that vv. 1-15 are generally a repetition of the ideas in chapter 15. In Robertson's commentary on John, he records this section to include 15:26-16:15.[76] The section comprising vv. 7-11 continues by expanding the discussion of the work of the Paraclete. Jesus assures the disciples that the Paraclete will not come unless He "goes away." Remember that Jesus Himself is the First Paraclete, the embodied Holy Spirit, and He must depart to the Father so that the Second Paraclete can appear.

Because the Second Paraclete is not limited to time and space, He can discern the hearts of men and assess their belief or unbelief. Thus He will serve as a judge (v. 8), convicting the world of its sin, and by such conviction, offer encouragement to the persecuted for Christ's sake. He will also be righteous in His judgment, echoing thoughts from the Old Testament.[77] Righteousness is not solely a moral attribute of the human spirit, but it is also inherent in the character of God. God is righteous; He is righteousness embodied, and He administers unbiased judgment to all

---

76. Robertson, *op. cit.,* 123.
77. See Psalm 7:17; 9:8; Isaiah 45:19.

men. He calls all men to righteousness and declares that the judgment of the Holy Spirit on men shall also be righteous.

The Second Paraclete, identical in nature to the First Paraclete, will reveal that the First Paraclete (Jesus) was, in point of fact, who He claimed to be, God's Son sent to be the Saviour of the world. The Holy Spirit will corroborate the life of Jesus as being who He said He was, God's Son. The Second Paraclete will further convict the world of judgment by exposing the invisible rulers of this evil world—Satan and his angels—and their overreach in crucifying the Lord of glory. This Second Paraclete will serve multiple purposes, but He will be a Paraclete not embodied as Jesus was embodied but a spiritual being, and He will come when Jesus departs.

Jesus Foretells His Death and Resurrection, 16:16-33

In vv. 16-17 Jesus prophetically foretells His death and resurrection. The "little while" of v. 16 refers to that time between His death on the cross and His reappearance to the disciples following the resurrection. This "intercorporis" describes the period during which Jesus' body would be changed from that of an earthly presence which the disciples had always known to a glorified, more spiritual existence. Jesus did not have human form post-resurrection.

Does this mean that He did not bodily resurrect? No, but His bodily form did change during this period of time from a common, material form to a glorified, transcendent reality. His "new body" would be evident upon His reappearance to the disciples, 20:19.

The time was approaching when the Son of Man would be "lifted up" and the unbelieving world would rejoice in a victory over apostasy. At the same time, the disciples would experience intense sorrow over the death of their Master. But that sorrow would be short-lived. That sorrow would soon be turned once again to joy.

The disciples remain "in the dark" with respect to their knowledge of who Jesus really is. He talked about being the Son of Man and the Son of God, but they could not fully comprehend who he was. He offered answers to their questions but often in mysterious language. Now, Jesus offers a condition and says, "when I am glorified," v. 14. When the term "glorified" is employed, it refers to the crucifixion and resurrection of Jesus. When He has accomplished the mission for which the Father sent Him, then they, and we, can ask the Father anything in His name and receive an answer, vv. 23-24.

Is Jesus referring to prayer? His statement allows for the inclusion of prayer after He has returned to the Father. Anything asked of the Father, however, must be in the name of the Son. So, does God answer every petition offered in the name of Jesus? The answer given by Jesus Himself is "yes." But the caveat "in My name" is critical to this verse. The Father will not answer those entreaties that are not offered in the name of the Son.

Be reminded that, while God will answer all petitions made in the name of Jesus, His answer does not always correspond to our human desires. God knows far more than our minds can conceive. He knows the future; He knows what is best for us, and His answers to our prayers will always be in our best interest, even if we cannot recognize His answers as such.

The evening in the Upper Room concludes with Jesus' profound words, words that the disciples would not fully grasp until the resurrection, vv. 25-33. Jesus was not unaware of His efforts, during His ministry, to teach the disciples. Yet he knew that the time approached when He would endure every conceivable disgrace and torture, yet they, His closest and dearest friends would utterly fail Him.

When they finally "got it," i. e., ultimately understood the meaning of the cross and the resurrection, they too would endure similar disgrace and torture. Jesus never promised that their lives or ours would be free from the experiences of misfortune or distress, but He did promise to lead them and us through the worst of those experiences. Jesus said, "be courageous"—a favorite word of His. That is a faith that cannot be diminished; that is a Master worth following.

Tenth Manifestation: The Great High Priestly Prayer, 17:1-26

Chapter 17 comprises the final or tenth manifestation of Jesus and is one of the most moving passages in John's Gospel. Originally designated as the "High Priestly Prayer of Jesus" by David Chytraeus,[78] the Father of Lutheranism who died in AD 1600, it is the "real" Lord's Prayer. Unlike the prayer of Matthew 6, Jesus did not have to pray for forgiveness, thus the Matthean prayer is better designated as the "model prayer." It is also appropriately termed the High Priestly Prayer because the Son of Man dedicates Himself to the mission to which the Father has called Him, namely His perfect sacrifice for the sins of mankind. He follows His own consecration with that of the disciples that they too may be offered in the service of perfect obedience to the call of God to win the world for Him. Although this prayer is spoken aloud as though the crucifixion and the resurrection were history, there is a tone of victory in it.

The prayer can be divided into three distinct sections: 1) Jesus' prayer for Himself, vv. 1-8; 2) Jesus' prayer for

78. Jonathan F. Bayes, *The Apostles' Creed: Truth with Passion*, Eugene, Oregon: Wipf & Stock, 2010, 143.

His disciples, vv. 9-19; and 3) Jesus' prayer for the church universal, vv. 20-26.

Unlike His statements to this point, Jesus knows that His "hour has come," that is, the "hour" of His glorification, His crucifixion. This "hour" is now at hand, and He is more than aware of that fact. His acknowledgment of the immediate future and His sacrifice form a fitting introduction to the section of the prayer with respect to Himself. The Son, whom men have despised and rejected, is now to be exalted as Lord.

Jesus prays specifically for the work which he was commissioned to do, vv. 1-8. His prayer includes two petitions for Himself: 1) That He may so render an account of His stewardship that the Father will be glorified through Him, exalted as a result of His sacrifice. Glory is the outward manifestation of the inner reality in Him, and through Him, the Father is to be glorified. He petitions the Father to confirm that He has accomplished the mission for which He was sent into the world. For this reason, the prayer is styled with the idea that the crucifixion had already occurred. 2) That His action throughout the suffering and death that will follow, will grant eternal life "for those You have given Me."

Eternal life, the ultimate end to faith in Christ is knowledge of God. In v. 3 Jesus unmistakably asserts that eternal life is "that they may know You, the only true God." To know in one's heart that God is and Jesus is His Son issues in eternal life. Eternal life simply is not a life of timelessness, although timelessness is a characteristic of it, but eternal life means being face to face with the Father of the universe; we are in the presence of the only True God. Acknowledgment of the Father and recognition of Jesus Christ as Him whom the Father sent into the world for its salvation issues a guarantee of eternal life. The name

"Jesus Christ," used only here and in 1:17, suggests that this one sentence describes the epitome of the Christian faith and its ultimate and eternal reality.

Many people view this concept of "everlasting life" only as a timeframe. But such is not the idea here. Eternal life is spoken of as being present, here and now, as well as future. I recall a church member of some years ago standing in a worship service and praying, "Lord, save us at last in heaven." I often thought about how confused his theology must be until I studied the Scriptures more fully and learned that he was correct. Eternal life begins now, but it comes to its completeness only when we come face to face with the Master.

From eternal life to bold contentions, Jesus claims three acknowledgments in the remainder of the verses about Himself. The first, v. 4, is that He was faithful to glorify the Father while on earth. Jesus created the church which will continue the work of glorifying the Father and the Son, but it all began with Jesus obeying His Father and fulfilling His mission to bring glory to the Him. In this prayer He acknowledges that He has been true to His purpose.

The second claim of Jesus is found in v. 6, "I have revealed Your name to the men You gave me from the world." Jesus faithfully exemplified the qualities of the Father before those whom He had called, and they were faithful, in turn, to accept His claim as the Son of God in spite of the world's influence to believe otherwise.

The third claim of these verses is v. 8, where Jesus said, "The words that You gave Me, I have given them." What a confirmation on behalf of the disciples! Here Jesus honors His disciples by conceding that they could have deserted Him, assuming Him to be simply another false prophet. But they did not abandon Him. Their hearts and minds were filled with His message, and, through the church, they would become a vessel poured out on His behalf to an unbelieving world. They were more than groupies, they genuinely trusted, by faith, in His Sonship. "They recognized that His mission was Divine: they believed that He was sent as the Messiah. They had proof of the first point; the second was a matter of faith."[79]

Jesus now turns His attention to His disciples, vv. 9-19. One can envision the passion of Jesus as He lifts His disciples to the Father. He prays that God will guard them as they continue to minister in His name, that the Father will protect them by His gracious providence so that they may be unified in their hearts and minds, like the mind of God.

Notice in v. 11 that Jesus pleads that the Father will "protect them by Your name." Remember how, in these times, names represented the essence of a person, one's character, one's inner, real self. Here, the "name" stands for the "personal power and character of God,"[80] the "I AM" who was and is and is to be. Jesus beseeches the Father to protect them, in life and in death.

Jesus also prays, in vv. 11-14, for the indivisible unity of His disciples. This unity will be further explored in vv. 22-23.

The practicality of Jesus' thought arises when, in vv. 15-16, He prays that, while they are in the world, they will not be of the world. Jesus prays that they will be shielded from the Evil One so that he will have no power over them. Such security can only come from the power of God, outside the forces of evil and the devil. They were to live in the world and enjoy it and yet not bow down to it or be swept away headlong by the influences of it. Jesus wanted them to enjoy all the good that life had to offer, but He wanted them to do so without being influenced by the standards of the world. A delicate balance, indeed! But this is also the life

79. Plummer, *op. cit.,* 311.
80. Buttrick, *op. cit.,* 747.

to which He calls us. Jesus prays for the assurance that the Father will strengthen them in this course.

Jesus appeals to the Father for their sanctification, vv. 17-19, that they may be made holy in the truth. They are to be dedicated, separated and set aside in the truth. What is the truth? It is the λόγος (*logos*), the Word of God. We know from the beginning verses of this Gospel that the *logos* incorporates God the Father and the Son in unity. Christ is the *logos* and their sanctification, their holification, will be made possible through His death. Jesus prays, therefore, that they will be true to Him, that they will be equipped by remaining steadfast in the truth that He has conveyed to them not only by their lips but also by the life of their Master.

After lifting supplications on His own behalf and that of His disciples, Jesus prays for the universal church, all believers everywhere, vv. 20-24, and the unity of the Body. His own disciples had demonstrated a lack of love and unity on this very night when they argued about who would be first in the Kingdom. Jesus takes this opportunity, not to ask the Father for union of thought but unity, a oneness of spirit.

Jesus intercedes on behalf of the church which has yet to be established (vv. 20-26), so He is actually referring to the church of the future, imploring that all believers may be one. He speaks of true ecumenicity and the universality of the purpose of God. Not lost in this prayer is the unity that exists between the Father and the Son, a unity of purpose that should also be the unifying force among fellow Christians everywhere. The common thread woven through the fabric of the church is to be oneness—true and faithful—with Him who sanctified the church and who is also one with the Father.

The common bond of Christ not only binds us as a faith community but also motivates us to share that bond with the world. Jesus speaks in v. 23, "so the world may know

You have sent me." Jesus' mission was to bring the world salvation; it is now the charge of believers to continue the work of the Son of God through their lives and ministry.

Jesus closes the prayer by shifting His tone from that of intercession and faith to hope. Some scholars have suggested that the tenor of this portion of Scripture and the prayer is purely eschatological because it illustrates a vision of the church glorified.

Jesus prays with no lack of clarity that even before the foundation of the world[81] God manifested His love to the Son, and now all who believe in the Son through faith and trust will have the love of the Father revealed in them. The world has rejected this love, v. 25, but God's love will continue through the work of the church. Jesus will continue His revelation through the Holy Spirit so that our knowledge and love of Christ may be one in the fellowship of life eternal.

John, the Gospeler, no doubt, considered this prayer as the perpetual prayer of the victorious and glorified Christ. He viewed it in its historical milieu of the Upper Room and closely connected it with the actions and words of Jesus while supping with His disciples.

The High Priestly Prayer of Jesus in the Upper Room speaks to the glorification, manifestation and sanctification of the church. The clarion call of Jesus on that night when He was betrayed was for His disciples, yea all believers, because He prayed for Himself, His disciples and you and me. What powerful words! He was thinking of you and me when He prayed that prayer. He prayed that we would be consecrated for service by following His example (glorification) and to be dedicated to the mission which He began.

Soon Christ will be with them no more and yet He will remain with them in Spirit. They have observed His

81. Reminiscent of 1:1 and 8:58.

ministry, but that ministry shall end, and He will no longer be with them physically. While He may not be seen with the eyes, He will forever be felt by His Spirit. The church is called to take up this mantle of evangelism (manifestation) and to spread the love of Christ by word and example. Jesus ordered the church, following His earthly ministry, to teach, worship, defend, sustain and replicate the kind of consecration He exhibited in His death and resurrection. On this mission rests the hope of ultimate glory.

Chapter Eight
John 18:1 – 19:41

Preparations for the Final Sign, 18:1-27

T he first eleven verses of this chapter depart, in several
instances, from the descriptions of the Synoptics.
Jesus has now departed the Upper Room and made His
way through the Valley (or Wadi, a dry riverbed) of Kidron
to a place not unfamiliar to the disciples, including Judas,
whom the Jewish leaders perceived to have inconsequential
allegiance to Him. Little wonder that the proxies of the
High Priest, his manipulators, bribed Judas and selected a
place for the arrest that was frequented by Jesus but not
commonly visited by the populace, especially at this time
of the evening. At this point the various descriptions vary.
Matthew and Mark indicate that Jesus took only Peter,
James and John with Him to the Garden of Gethsemane.
Both Luke and John note that He took "the disciples,"
indicating possibly the entire group of Eleven. Such an
account would support the possibility, at least, that a
portion of the previous discourses may have taken place
in the Garden.

In all three Synoptics, Jesus is shown to have asked His disciples to sit and wait as He prayed. In Matthew and Mark, He asked them only to wait[82] while He prayed. Nowhere in John do we find a reference either to His instructions to His disciples to wait or His prayer in the Garden.

The Synoptics also refer to Judas leading a "multitude" that included a group of leaders from the Jews, but only John writes that he "received"[83] the "band of soldiers," implying them to be Roman, accompanied by Jewish representatives. The band of soldiers, whose armament is described in Matthew and Mark only, likely were from the legion billeted nearby at the tower of Antonia. Carrying lanterns, torches and weapons, the "band" probably did not consist of a complete cohort or battalion which would have comprised 500 or more men, rather it was most likely a platoon mustered from among the battalion at Antonia for the purpose of maintaining peace during the Feast of Passover.

The soldiers were accompanied by a group of temple police. Matthew states that the Jewish contingent included chief priests and elders, officials of the Temple. Mark adds scribes to this list, but Luke mentions only that a crowd approached Jesus. John writes a somewhat more detailed description by adding that the Jewish element of the crowd consisted of "officers of the chief priests" and "Pharisees." So they were not the chief priests, elders and scribes themselves but only their representatives. John's version might be more accurate since the chief priests or the Pharisees personally would not have desired to have been named as conspirators against Jesus. They wished to claim as much innocence as possible and work behind the scenes

---

82. This word can also be translated as "keep awake" or be "vigilant."

83. This is the translation of the New American Standard Version. The Greek can also mean "get together with."

to carry out the dastardly deed and let their representatives do the dirty work. So they sent their agents who comprised a kind of "temple police" force to accompany the soldiers to meet Jesus.

Another difference among the Gospels includes the cutting off of the slave's ear in all four Gospels, but only in John do we learn the name of the perpetrator. His purpose for naming Peter is unknown. But the greater question might be, Why was Peter armed in the first place? Was the entire disciple band armed? Is their being armed the reason for a large contingent of soldiers? These are questions that cannot be answered by a study of the text alone. They beg a much larger question not to be discussed here.

John writes of no evidence in the text that Jesus offered to or actually did heal the ear of the centurion.[84] Perhaps John supposed that any writing with respect to the healing of the soldier's ear might be deemed as yet another "sign," and he did not intend another "sign" to be so apparent that the final "sign" yet to come would not effectually point to Jesus' appointed "hour."

Nowhere are the powers of darkness better enumerated than by John during the arrest of Jesus in the Garden. These powers of darkness were represented by 1) one from among His own disciple band, Judas, 2) the civil authorities, i. e., Roman soldiers, and 3) the religious leaders who sought to destroy Him.

Notice how the power of Jesus can and does ultimately overcome these earthly forces of darkness. When Jesus responded to their question by saying, "I am He," the group fell to the ground. Why? Did they recognize that this man was indeed the innocent deliverer of a message of peace and love? Were they struck guilty by the power of the

---

84. In Luke 22:51 Jesus is described as having healed the ear of the soldier.

will of God in the presence of the Son of Man? Were they afraid? We have no way of knowing, but their response was unexpected.

A final textual variance relates to the kiss of Judas. Matthew and Mark mention that Judas kissed Jesus as was prescribed in Judas' agreement with the Jewish authorities. Luke mentions that Judas approached Jesus to kiss Him, but there is no indication that he actually did because, before Judas can complete the act, Jesus asks him a question, "Judas, are you betraying the Son of Man with a kiss?"[85] The Gospeler abbreviates the entire event by not including either a kiss or the betrayal. John wished to advance the narrative as quickly as possible to proceed to the important final "sign" and to heighten the idea that Jesus volunteered Himself.

Jesus Before the Jewish Authorities and Peter's Denial, 18:12-27

The Gospels present some difficulty in understanding precisely who, among the Jewish authorities, actually condemned Jesus. The Synoptic narratives record that Jesus was brought only before Caiaphas, the High Priest and that he questioned Jesus about His disciples and His teachings. John, however, records that Jesus was first brought to Annas, the father-in-law of Caiaphas. Annas, a Sadducee, was an ex-High Priest, having served AD 7-14, but when he retired from the position, he kept the powerful post in the family. John's reference to the "the high priest's courtyard" may simply be a respectful reference to Annas as a high profile former Jewish supreme leader. Matthew, Mark and John agree that the trial took place at night, offering a kind of sinister conspiracy.

---

85. Luke 22:48.

The text of the Gospel of John may be reversed with respect to Jesus' appearances for questioning. A preliminary examination of Jesus was likely conducted by Annas as shown in vv. 19-23. The reference to the High Priest in v. 19 probably refers to the common usage of the day to a former High Priest much as we would continue to call a former president "Mr. President." Then in v. 24, Jesus is turned over to Caiaphas for final questioning before deliverance to the Roman authorities.

Why did Annas query Jesus about His teachings? The most practical reason would be the fear that the New Order (Christianity) would pose a real threat to the Jewish establishment. Annas did not wish for the *status quo* to be jeopardized. Jesus' response to the questioning is quite open and honest. He denies any efforts to destabilize the Jewish order or to conceive and execute plans of a political nature that might intimidate the Roman government. While true, Jesus's statements were unsettling to the former High Priest, and he sent Him on to Caiaphas.

Beginning in v. 17 John unfolds the narrative of Peter's denial. Peter was denied entrance into the court of the High Priest until John, an acquaintance of the High Priest, intervened on his behalf. So the scene is set for the denial.

Peter's first repudiation of Jesus came at the hands of a slave girl, a "portress," who kept the door to the court of the High Priest, the room where Jesus was appearing. Her question to Peter seems to come from an earlier sighting of him with Jesus. Peter's denying response is both immediate and unequivocal.

Since John was an acquaintance of the High Priest, the doorkeeper-slave girl probably also recognized him from earlier contact. Departing to the quadrangle, Peter joins himself to a group of slaves who were standing with several of the soldiers who executed the arrest of Jesus.

They were warming themselves in front of a fire. There Peter stands shedding the coldness of his body but adding coldness to his spirit.

After an interruption of the story, a kind of pericope (vv. 19-24), John returns to Peter in v. 25. Peter remains standing at the fire when the soldiers asked him about his relationship with Jesus. Once again, denial.

After a third denying response to a slave of the High Priest, the cock crows. Peter has been faithful, strong, forthright and supportive, and Jesus had said, "Even in your faithfulness you will deny me." Peter could not envision such an act. "Not going to happen Lord."

What could be going through his mind when he hears that cock crow? Peter suddenly grasps the import of his actions and the prophesying words of Jesus. His shame is overpowering; we are told in the Synoptics[86] that he departed and wept inconsolably and repentantly. Peter went from the mountaintop to the valley, all in one evening!

Although John writes that Jesus appeared before Caiaphas, he offers no details, not charges or an indictment. All that we might know about his trial before Caiaphas will be found in the Synoptics. John's focus was not on the trial but the "sign" that was yet to come.

Jesus Before the Roman Authorities, 18:28-19:16

From the beginning John has been recognized as a dramatist of extraordinary skill. He has employed drama throughout his Gospel to heighten the intensity of the story, to accentuate the emotional impact of certain events and to drive home the significance of faith in standing with Jesus, who he believed to be, declared to be and wanted to prove to be the Christ.

86. Matthew 26:75; Mark 14:72; Luke 22:62.

Once again, John introduces the dramatic element in the final hours of Jesus' life. The appearance of Jesus before the Roman authorities and the reactions of the Jews provide an apt setting for his version of the trial. It occurs in seven scenes, a number not lost on the Jews.

The first scene (18:28-32) takes place early in the morning[87] just outside the Praetorium, the official residence of Pilate, the Roman Prefect. Jews would not enter the Praetorium, the home of a Gentile, lest they be defiled and by such defilement could not partake of the Passover meal. So they stood outside and awaited Pilate's presence. When he appeared, he inquired about the charge that the Jews were making against Jesus, v. 29.

The Jews could not articulate a specific charge, only that he was some kind of agitator, v. 30. With no specific charge, Pilate would release Jesus to the Jews for prosecution. But the Jews were not empowered by the Romans to put anyone to death. Even so, execution by the Jews was stoning while that of the Romans was crucifixion, the method prophesied as the sacrifice of the Messiah. The Jews refused to accept him.

Scene two (18:33-38a) opens in v. 33 with Pilate returning to the Praetorium and having Jesus brought inside. Here he questions Jesus with respect to His kingship. An interesting query! Pilate's question presupposes that Jesus has something of a kingly quality, a kingly character, but in no way does He appear outwardly like a king. He did not look like a king; He did not act like a king; He did not speak like a king; He did not carry His authority like a king, but Pilate was not dismissive of the possibility that He was a king. The subject of the scene juxtaposes the nature of the heavenly kingdom against that of an earthly kingdom.

---

87. Probably just before sunrise.

Jesus makes clear that His kingdom is not of this world. It is not a kingdom with armies and navies to defend it; it is not a kingdom of governance and politics; it is not even a kingdom of human origin. These words must have puzzled Pilate as evidenced by his asking the question again in v. 37. Only here do we find the Greek οὐκοῦν (*oukoun*, "so" or "then") in the New Testament. By adding to this term the pronoun σύ (*su*, "you"), Pilate disrespects Jesus. Plummer writes that the response of Pilate "gives a tone of scorn to the question."[88]

Jesus' words in v. 37 are reminiscent of both the Prologue to the Gospel and His words in 14:6 when He stated "I am the truth." Jesus bore witness of the truth, His Father, and, as an ambassador of the Father, is Himself ultimate truth. Belief in Him ushers in an eternal quality of existence that cannot be understood by either Pilate or any man.

Pilate's inquiry in v. 38, "What is truth?" may be a rhetorical question with no intellectual intent behind it. Or it may have been Pilate's attempt to engage Jesus in an intellectual debate. In either case, notice the absence of the article. He did not ask to know "the" truth, only "truth." He may simply have been curious about how Jesus would respond or he, perhaps, may actually have been serious in his inquiry. More likely the question was asked in derision and jest. In any case, Jesus posed no seditious threat to the Roman Empire, and Pilate recognized that fact. So not wishing to be placed in a compromising position, Pilate satiated the Jews' thirst for blood. As reported by Hoskyns, "It was the blasphemous activity of the Jews, not the convictions of Pilate, which led him to the decision that Jesus should be crucified."[89]

---

88. Plummer, *op. cit.,* 333.
89. Hoskyns, *op. cit.,* 521.

Scene three (18:38b-40) begins as Pilate returned to the outer courtyard. Here the Gospeler writes the first of three declarations of Pilate with respect to Jesus' innocence, v. 38. Pilate wanted no part in this illegal scheme and wished to release Him. The Jews would have no part of it. They were determined to succeed in their murderous intent.

Pilate sees a way out by invoking a practice of releasing a prisoner at Passover. By imposing this practice, he can release Jesus. But the crowd, excited and seeking blood because of the incitement by the Jewish ecclesiastics, calls for the release of Barabbas, a λῃστής (*lēstēs*), a word which describes a robber, a bandit, a plunderer or even a revolutionary.[90] He, indeed, would incite riots and rebellion against the Roman Empire. Barabbas was not a nice person. He was in fact an insurrectionist who had rebelled against Rome, a fact not lost on Roman authorities. What a striking contrast to the humility and sincerity of Jesus! Pilate now had a hard decision to make.

Believing that he might find a way to assuage the Jews, Pilate opens scene four (19:1-3) by having Jesus scourged. The text would imply that Jesus remained inside the Praetorium where He was beaten, although He likely was taken outside. Normally the flagellation, both demeaning and brutal, would have been preparatory to crucifixion, however, the Gospeler includes it here as yet another attempt by Pilate either to convince the Jews to let Him go or to force Jesus to confess to a sin against the state.

When the scourging did not have the desired effect, Pilate turned Jesus over to his soldiers who took Jesus' words at face value and mocked Him by bedecking Him with a faded purple robe and a crown of thorns. Such

---

90. William F. Arndt and F. Wilbur Gingrich, *A Greek-English Lexicon of the New Testament*, Chicago: University of Illinois Press, 1957, 474.

regalia would naturally adorn a "king." Matthew 27:30 and Mark 15:19 describe the soldiers as spitting in mock victory over a vanquished foe, however, John focuses on the assault of Jesus by the soldiers who took turns slapping Him with their hands. The humiliation continued.

Scene five (19:4-7) includes perhaps the most dramatic overture to be written in the pre-crucifixion narratives. For a second time, Pilate declares that he finds nothing for which Jesus is guilty, v. 4. But the pressure on Pilate is building.

Found only here in John's Gospel, this dramatic portrayal might best be identified as the "ecce homo" passage. These Latin words are derived from the Vulgate (Latin) translation of the Greek Ἰδοὺ ὁ ἄνθρωπος (*Idou ho anthrōpos*), "behold (look at) the man." Pilate's declaration was not a spiritual pronouncement. He did not announce, "Behold the Son of God"; or "Behold the Lamb of God"; or even "Behold God." His announcement was one of derision, designed to proclaim to the Jews that this man was nothing more than a mere mortal who did not have it in Him to oppose the power and authority of Rome.

Jesus is brought from inside the Praetorium to the outer courtyard where He is on display before the crowd of Jews. Inflamed by the chief priests, the crowd shouts in chorus, "Crucify." Convinced by the Jewish ecclesiastics that He is a blasphemer, they call out, "Crucify."

In the latter part of v. 6, Pilate gives them tacit permission to take Him and crucify Him. But this approval is, in fact, a mockery standing on its own. Yet, for the third time, he announces that he finds "no guilt in Him." He did not have any intention of releasing Jesus to them, but the weight of their words in v. 7, which he now heard for the first time, struck fear in his heart. Jesus had claimed divinity, a blasphemy punishable by death. But one fact remained: prophecy. He could not be stoned according to the Jewish law, even though it was the Jewish Law that he allegedly had violated. He must be crucified—prophecy.

Jesus and Pilate return to the Praetorium for scene six (19:8-11). The scene contrasts the authority of Jesus with that of Pilate. Pilate queries Jesus about His identity. Probably expecting Jesus to respond that He was from Nazareth or Bethlehem or Galilee, the question is met only with silence. Why respond when he who is inquiring is incapable of comprehending the truth? No accurate answer could be given to the question that would have satisfied Pilate. So, silence!

Pilate responds to the silence with imperial arrogance. But Jesus is unmoved and unimpressed. His answer to Pilate is a simple reminder that Pilate's power and authority to crucify or not to crucify Jesus is "from above." While Pilate is guilty of misusing his power, it is the guilt of the Jews who have delivered Him on a trumped up charge who possess the greater guilt.

The final scene in this drama is described in 19:12-16. Best titled "threat and delivery," these verses describe a cowardly Prefect whose concern for his career outweighed any moral obligation to this lowly Jew. After all, as Prefect, he did not wish to be viewed as being disloyal to Caesar, and since a "friend of Caesar's cannot also be the friend of Jesus,"[91] Pilate's choices were very limited.

Under threat from the Jews Pilate has Jesus brought once again to the outer courtyard. Scholars are divided as to the exact description that follows, specifically, whether Pilate sat on the throne—the judgment seat—or whether Pilate had Jesus sit on the throne. The Greek ἐκάθισεν (*ekathisen*) can be translated as a transitive verb meaning "to cause to sit." It can also be translated intransitively

91. Hoskyns, *op. cit.*, 524.

as "to sit." Being a consummate dramatist, it is likely that John deliberately heightens the drama of this scene by having Jesus enthroned upon the tribunal or judgment seat that was located in an area known as the λιθόστρωτον (*lithostrōton*), translated "Pavement."

By having Jesus sit on the throne Pilate would make even greater mockery of Jesus' self-declaration of kingship. The language of the picture itself would illustrate the "supremacy" of Pilate by having him stand over or above Jesus in the position of power and authority, one more demeaning portrait of the Lamb of God being humiliated and debased.

The area termed the "Pavement" was substantively a mosaic or tessellated pavement, a place near the Praetorium or palace where judgment was rendered. Jesus was forced to sit as a king in mocking derision as Pilate declares, unlike the words of 19:5, "Here is your King," v. 14.

The timing of this declaration and the delivery of Jesus is important not only to the structure of the events but also to the message of the narrative. The appearance before Pilate, i. e., Jesus' preparation for crucifixion, parallels the preparation for the Feast of Passover. At 6:00 a. m., on this day Jesus, the Lamb of God, is delivered to be crucified, not by the Jews but by the Romans. It is the Jews, however, that have demanded His execution; it is the Jews that have rejected Him as sovereign God; it is the Jews that have denied Him being the Messiah. He has come unto His own, and His own have received Him not.

The Seventh Sign: The Hour: Act 1, The Crucifixion, 19:17-24

The hour for the final "sign" has arrived. Jesus has been "tried" before the Roman Prefect, Pilate, and has been ordered to be crucified. The Gospeler begins his account of the crucifixion by emphasizing the fact that Jesus bore His own cross. Two possible reasons might explain why he focused on this part of the narrative. 1) John wished to show that Jesus was treated just as any other common criminal might have been treated when being executed. Jesus was not specially treated; every criminal bore his own cross to the place of execution. 2) A Gnostic version of the story was circulated following the crucifixion claiming that Jesus was not truly put to death. Rather, Simon of Cyrene, mentioned in the Synoptics and who had been forced to carry Jesus' cross, was actually the person who was crucified.[92] By omitting any reference to Simon, John wished to make clear that Jesus was, indeed, the One put to death that day, along with two common thieves.

According to all four Gospels, Jesus is forced to drag His cross to the outskirts of Jerusalem where these executions regularly occurred. Probably located reasonably near the city, it was known as Golgotha, the place of the skull, due to its prominent skull-like appearance. There He is crucified between two other men, making Jesus the focal character in this sadistic tragedy.

All four Gospels describe a written inscription placed atop the cross, however, each Gospel writer has inscribed it differently. It was the general practice of the Roman government to use a white chalky substance like gypsum to write on a crude piece of wood that was attached to a cross to proclaim the reason why a person was being executed. Matthew writes (27:37), "This is Jesus the King of the Jews." Mark simplifies the inscription (15:26) by

---

92. This version can be found in the writings of Irenaeus, *Against Heresies*, XXIV, 4, as written in Alexander Roberts', *The Ante-Nicene Fathers*, The Christian Literature Publishing Company, 1885.

writing only, "The King of the Jews." Luke (23:38) states, "This is the King of the Jews."

John's purpose is more fittingly achieved by taking a slightly wordier approach to the inscription, v. 19, "Jesus the Nazarene, the King of the Jews." Three unique characteristics emerge from this inscription. First, John does not use the word for "inscription," rather he writes that it was a τίτλον (*titlon*). While this word can be translated as "inscription," it is more in keeping with John's purpose that it be translated in its original form as "title." That is, Pilate placed a sign on the cross of Jesus that would both state the charge and offer derisive contempt for this man, a Nazarene, who dared to claim kingship.

Second, John is the only Gospel writer to designate Jesus' hometown of Nazareth in Galilee as a part of the inscription. While contempt on the part of Pilate played a role in this wording, was it also an attempt on the part of Pilate to further irritate the Jews by declaring that Jesus was one of them? Perhaps, but it may also have been reminiscent of 1:46 when Nathaniel said, "Can anything good come out of Nazareth."

Third, the inscription was written in three languages, Latin, Greek and Hebrew (Aramaic). The unique mentioning of these three languages illustrates the practices of the day. Latin was the official language of the Roman Empire representing human government, strength and authority. It was employed in all governmental decrees and orders.

Greek was the language of the economy and of society in general. It was the international language of a cultured and civilized society. It represented art, intelligence, wisdom, and business.

Hebrew, more commonly known as Aramaic, was the language of the streets among the Palestinian Jews. It was the religious language of the Jews and represented the

Covenant Race, the Law of God, and the means by which God made Himself known to man.[93] All could read and understand the charges. So on the cross of Jesus "meet the three chief civilizations of the world."[94] Christ's mission of universal salvation is complete.

Only in John do we learn the disposition of Jesus' garments. John likely included this part of the story to add credibility to his overall purpose (20:31). Earlier Jesus had been stripped of His outer clothing, leaving only His tunic, ὁ χιτὼν (*ho chitōn*). The Greek term refers to a garment worn next to the skin, thus it was more of an undergarment. His normal clothing had been replaced with a faded purple robe as a sign of His "kingship." However, His original garment was divided into four parts, with each soldier who obediently participated in His crucifixion being awarded a portion as a reward or keepsake.

After dividing His clothing among the quaternion responsible for carrying out the crucifixion, John notes that they ponder what to do with the undergarment or tunic. It was seamless, and since they had already divided His outer cloak, they decided to cast lots for it, completely unaware that, by doing so they fulfilled a prophecy found in Psalm 22:18, "They divide my garments among themselves, and they cast lots for my clothing." Yet another validation of John's purpose that Jesus was the Christ, the fulfillment of prophecy.

John may have included his description of these events as a way of pointing to Jesus as the Great High Priest. The High Priest was known to adorn himself with a seamless undergarment as a part of his ceremonial attire.[95] By referencing this piece of vesture he emphasized the High Priestly function of Jesus and His sacrificial act.

---

93. *Apologia* 3(2):17-18, 1994.
94. Robertson, *op. cit.*, 146.
95. See Josephus, *Antiquities*, Book III.

The Final Hours, 19:25-30

John includes little detail in the final hours of Jesus' life. At the Cross He describes only who was there and three sayings of Jesus from the Cross.

While the crowd surrounding the Cross comprised many people from the area, John only mentions Mary, the mother of Jesus, her sister, Mary the wife of Cleopas, Mary Magdalene and "they" of v. 29, assumed to be soldiers. Watching her son die insufferably, Mary must have been beyond distraught and grief-stricken. It is at this moment that Jesus looks upon her and says one of the three quotations revealed by John in v. 26, "Woman, here is your son."[96]

This saying of Jesus can be viewed from two perspectives. The first perspective is completely human and refers to Jesus' genuine concern for those closest to Him. In these last hours, when the emphasis is on the unearthliness of Jesus—His deity—Jesus was thinking of His mother and her well-being. He, therefore, commends her to the care of John the Beloved Disciple, not her son. What a tremendous display of His humanity!

Why would He not commend her to his brothers? First, they may not have been present at Calvary. Second, at this point in time His brothers remained as unbelievers and did not accept His assertion as being the Messiah. They did not arrive at a faith in His Messiahship until after the resurrection. John was like a brother to Jesus, and to commend her to him was an act honor and respect.

The second perspective is John's emphasis upon the symbolism of the moment. Theologically, Mary represents the Old Israel, the faith from which the New Israel, the

---

96. The use of the term "Woman," is the same Greek word employed in 2:4 at the wedding in Cana. It is a term of endearment meaning "lady," and expresses honor and respect.

ἐκκλησία (*ekklēsia*), the church, would emerge. John, the Beloved Disciple, whose belief in Jesus as the Christ, represents the New Israel and by commending Mary to him, Jesus now commends her to the house of one who represents the New Covenant. The Old Israel (in Mary) has given birth to a New Israel (in Jesus). She is placed in the care of John who represents the quintessential Christian (New Israel) and into whose care (in John) she has been placed.

He commends her to John who accepts the responsibility of caring for her. His relationship is to be one of such devotion that Jesus considers John to be her son, hence, "Here is your mother." Tradition has it that she remained in John's house until her death.

Yet another acknowledgment of Jesus' humanity is displayed when He said, "I'm thirsty," v. 28. Hanging on the Cross exposed to the middle eastern sun naturally caused dehydration. As a man, Jesus would have become dehydrated like any other human being, and His desire for water would have been typical, but it also fulfilled the prophetic words of Psalm 69:21, "For my thirst they gave me vinegar to drink."

Three elements of this occurrence are worthy of comment. Note first that the soldiers used a sprig of hyssop to place some "sour wine" on the lips of Jesus. While Matthew and Luke employ the same word, ὄξος (*oxos*), it has generally been translated as "vinegar."[97] Other translations acknowledge the custom of the day when a vessel of old wine was positioned near the crucifixion site for the soldiers to imbibe while executing their orders. It is likely, therefore, that the offering was actually a portion of this sour wine. John records specifically that Jesus accepted the sour wine upon His lips.

97. See the King James Version and the Revised Standard Version.

A second element comprises the hyssop that was used to offer Jesus relief from His thirst. Matthew and Mark mention the use of a sponge placed upon a reed but do not specify the exact type of reed used. John also describes the use of a sponge but writes that it was placed upon hyssop as the means of offering the vinegar to Jesus for quenching His thirst. The word John chooses, ὕσσωπος (hussōpos), which means a branch or reed of hyssop, is one of the most widely used and valued herbs of the Palestinians.

Some scholars argue that the instrument used to convey the sour wine was actually a sponge[98] that was impaled on the tip of a Roman javelin. The argument is that the word actually written by John in his original manuscript was the word ὕσσος (hussos) which refers to a Roman javelin or spear. Thus the soldiers would have soaked a sponge in the vessel of sour wine, attached it to the end of a spear and lifted it to Jesus' lips. While such an action is possible, it is more likely that an actual branch of hyssop was applied.

The reason for such a conclusion comprises the third element of this portion of the crucifixion story. Hyssop, an herb in the mint family with cleansing, medicinal, and flavoring properties, was prolific in the Middle East and was used in a variety of ways. It is referenced in ten places in the Old Testament, e. g., when referring to ceremonial cleansing from skin disease (Leviticus 14) as well as the red heifer offering (Numbers 19). It is also referenced as a purging agent when David mentioned hyssop in Psalm 51:7, "Purify me with hyssop, and I will be clean." Its most vital ceremonial use was at the time of the Passover (Exodus 12:22). God commanded the Israelites to take a hyssop branch and smear the blood of sacrificed animals upon the lintels of

---

98. In keeping with the Matthean and Markan accounts of the crucifixion.

each home so that the Death Angel would pass, leaving the firstborn untouched. The hyssop symbolically, therefore, points to Jesus as both the Lamb of God in His Passover death and the Door, which He declared Himself to be, both images that emerge from the deliverance story.

With Christ represented as the Paschal Lamb whose blood issues forgiveness of sin, the hyssop is a symbol used by John to legitimize the cleansing power of Jesus' sacrifice. John is reminding the reader that there is no forgiveness of sin without the shedding of innocent blood.[99] It was that principle that reminded the Jews of their deliverance from four hundred years of bondage in Egypt. John is writing that the sacrifice of Jesus is a reminder of the Jewish Day of Atonement when the priest would enter the Holy of Holies and use a hyssop branch to spread the blood of calves and goats upon and in front of the Ark of the Covenant for the forgiveness of sin. The hyssop branch becomes a "sign" within a "sign" that this One, whose blood is required for the purification of sin is also Him to whom the Israelites paid homage for the passage of the Passover Angel. Jesus sheds the innocent blood for mankind once and for all.

The final words recorded by John as spoken by Jesus from the Cross, "It is finished," v. 30, fit perfectly into his narrative and purpose for writing. John's is the only Gospel to record these words.

John writes that Jesus said, "It," a neutral pronoun with no antecedent. To what does this pronoun refer? Jesus came to earth with a specific mission from the Father, and His greatest desire was to fulfill that mission. Now, on the Cross, thirty-three years later, His "hour" has come for that mission to reach its conclusion.

"Finished," He cried out. Such a declaration might have been interpreted as referring to the ebbing away of His

99. Leviticus 17:11

physical life, but such would not have been consistent with John's purpose in writing it. The Greek term τελέω (teleō) used here by Jesus means to end or accomplish. The verb form, τετέλεσται (tetelestai), is the third person singular, indicative, passive which does not refer to a chronological end but to a qualitative, substantive completion. By this declaration Jesus does not bring His life to an end, but rather He affirms that His work as the ὁ λόγος σὰρξ ἐγένετο (ho logos sarx egeneto), "the Word became flesh," is completed in the Cross.

"It is finished" is a cry of triumph, an affirmation of the defeat of good over evil, an exclamation of "mission accomplished." Jesus confirmed His death to be the beginning of the end, not the end of the beginning.[100] The work of Redemption is now complete.

Crucifixion Practices and Prophecy, 19:31-37

The evening is fast approaching and the condemned are perceived as not dead yet. To the Jews, this presented a problem. According to the Deuteronomic Code (Deuteronomy 21:23), a dead body could not be left on a cross overnight. Additionally, it was Friday, the day for preparation for both the Sabbath and the Passover Feast. These men, especially Jesus, must be dead and buried before sunset.[101]

As a part of common practice the legs of the condemned were to be broken in order to inflict more pain and hasten death. In this case, however, the Jews were less

---

100. Strachan, op. cit., 321.

101. The race or nationality of the two criminals crucified with Jesus is not known. If not Jews, then the ecclesiastics would have no concern with the disposition of their bodies, but Jesus, being a Jew, must be in the grave by sunset.

concerned about the two criminals than they were the disposition of Jesus' body. So the Romans complied with the Jewish request that the legs of these men be broken, only because they were concerned that they keep the religious laws relating to Jesus.

So the Roman soldiers proceeded to break the legs of the condemned. Why did the soldiers wait to break the legs of Jesus last? Why did they simply not break the legs of them in order? As professional executioners, they were in no hurry; they were likely drunk from the sour wine and did not take care with the order in which the legs were broken. Or was it simply that God was in control, even in the crucifixion?

For whatever reason unknown to the reader of the Gospel, after completing the task with the other two criminals, they found that Jesus was already dead. It would not be necessary to break His legs so as to fulfil the prophecy of Numbers 9:12 and Psalm 34:20. The time is 3:00 p. m., Nisan 14,[102] the day and hour at which the Passover Lamb was customarily slain. John sees in Jesus the Lamb of God, slain on that very afternoon at the exact time.

Found nowhere else in the Gospels, John includes one last indignity inflicted upon Jesus. Unconscious of the fulfillment of prophecy found in Zechariah 12:10[103], one of the soldiers took up his lance (spear) and pierced the side of Jesus. Immediately the gaping wound issues forth blood and water. The collection of blood and water in the tissues would have naturally been a result of puncturing

102. See Matthew 27:46, Mark 15:34 and Luke 23:44.
103. The Lord God speaks: "Then I will pour out a spirit of grace and prayer on the house of David and the residents of Jerusalem, and they will look at Me whom they pierced. They will mourn for Him as one mourns for an only child, and weep bitterly for Him as one weeps for a firstborn."

a dead, swollen body. Perhaps John added these details to dispute the claims of the Docetic Gnostics that Jesus did not actually die but swooned in unconsciousness. Thus the Gnostics could not declare His resurrection as being impossible. Rather, John describes in morbid detail the gushing forth of water and blood that would have signaled sure death.

While John's purpose may have included defying the Gnostics, he surely had a higher purpose in mind. The spurting forth of the blood and water possessed a more spiritual significance for the Gospeler. For John all mankind is possessed of life, water and spirit. At the moment that Jesus announced the completion of His task, His spirit departed. Reminiscent of the establishment of the first covenant as described in Hebrews,[104] the water that poured forth from His wound represented the water of birth (amniotic fluid) and the water of Jesus' baptism through which His obedience to the Father was professed.

The blood that surged forth symbolized His life, offered voluntarily for the sins of all mankind. Jesus was not coerced to accept His mission. He knew what that mission was to be from early in life, and He accepted the Father's will and did so voluntarily. On the Cross, the gushing forth of His blood represents that life obediently and freely given for the sins of mankind.

Water and spirit came together in His baptism, water and blood flowed together at His death. But even in His death, Jesus is alive! And because He is alive, He is the Source of all life, even eternal life.

Verse 35 declares the truth of the event. John contested the Gnostics by an unnamed witness. This mysterious witness, who is likely the Beloved Disciple himself, confirmed the truth of these events. He witnessed both the

104. Hebrews 9:19

historical event and attested to its spiritual significance. Indeed, this One crucified, dead and buried was the Son of God! "I know because I witnessed it."

The Hour, Act 2, The Burial of Jesus, 19:38-41

In Act 2, the body of Jesus is handled in accordance with Jewish Law regarding dead bodies. The Deuteronomic Code required that the body be in the grave by sunset. Enter Joseph of Arimathea.

Joseph was an esteemed member of the Sanhedrin. Wealthy (Matthew 27:57), influential (Mark 15:43) and upright (Luke 23:50), he was from Arimathea, an undefined city in Judea. Out of fear for the actions of the Sanhedrin, he was a secret follower of Jesus, unwilling to open himself to the potential vengeance of the Jews and their ecclesiastical and fanatical leadership.

Joining him was another member of the Sanhedrin, Nicodemus, who was mentioned earlier in 3:1. Wealthy in his own right, Nicodemus supplied the spices and ointments necessary to prepare the body of Jesus for appropriate Jewish burial. The remarkable courage of both men, especially in light of their positions, is exhibited in their request to Pilate for Jesus' body.

John, and perhaps even Mary deep in grief, stood by as these two powerful and influential followers of the Nazarene prepared His body for burial. Only by being an eyewitness to this event could John have so carefully and meticulously described the process, how much aloe and spice was used and precisely how they wrapped Him. He also may have assisted, since more than two persons might have been required to lift or reposition the body of the Saviour as they would have done in the preparation.

After removing Jesus from the Cross, the two men wrapped Him in linen, pouring aloe and spices between the coverings. Once completely wrapped, He was ready for burial.

Nicodemus supplied one hundred Roman pounds or about 1200 ounces of spices necessary to accomplish the task for which they had requested Jesus' body. Why such a large quantity? John's mind could only envision Jesus as truly the "King of the Jews." The burial of Jesus was to be a kingly burial, deserving of royal treatment. Nicodemus' supply of these spices and ointments only confirmed the symbolism of John with respect to such a royal interment.

A speedy burial of Jesus was only made possible through the generosity of Joseph of Arimathea[105] who possessed a tomb in a garden near the spot of crucifixion in which no person had been buried. With only about three hours left in the Day of Preparation, they hastily made ready the body of Jesus in the traditional manner of burial and laid it to rest in the borrowed tomb.

John accounts for no mourners at the gravesite of Jesus. Perhaps they were scattered, going through the valley of the shadow of death, each in his own way. So ends Act 2 of this final sign.

---

105. Matthew 27:60

Chapter Nine
John 20:1 – Conclusion

The Hour, Act 3, The Final Sign: The Resurrection, 20:1-10

A ct three of this final "sign" that comprises the Passion of the Christ, opens on a daybreak scene at the tomb. Only in John do we find Mary Magdalene there, although the Synoptics describe other women as having accompanied her. She has appeared at the tomb perhaps to anoint the body of Jesus with preserving spices, perhaps simply to mourn the passing of her friend and spiritual mentor. In any case, she left home before dawn, arriving at the tomb soon after sunrise.

Upon arriving, Mary observed that the stone either had spontaneously rolled, by gravity, from the entrance to the tomb or had been deliberately rolled away by someone. The stone had been rolled away by the power of the risen Christ.

Note especially that Mary never actually entered the tomb. Seeing the stone removed, she assumed that someone had pilfered the body of Jesus or had secreted it away. Astonished and puzzled by what she witnessed, she leaves to tell Peter and the others what she has observed.

Upon hearing the news from Mary, Peter and John the Beloved Disciple ran to the tomb, John arriving first and peeking inside but not entering. What he saw shocked and bewildered him. Peter entered and was no less surprised at what he saw. There, lying rolled up and placed neatly upon the raised shelf where Jesus' head had lain, was the cloth that would have covered his face in death. It was not arbitrarily cast to one side as it might have been if thieves had stolen the body of Jesus, but it was methodically and meticulously rolled and placed upon the "head shelf."

The body wrappings that would have surrounded the physical body of Jesus were neither missing nor scattered about the tomb floor. Rather, they remained in the reclining position in which Jesus would have been buried, His bodily form still maintained. But the wrappings contained no physical body.

John's observation of the tomb and the condition of the wrappings convinced him that Jesus no longer lived in a physical body but had been transformed into a spiritual body. John's conviction is confirmed in v. 8 where the Gospeler writes, he "saw, and believed."

John writes in v. 9 that the disciples did not understand the Scripture. Jesus had alluded to His death and resurrection on several occasions during His ministry, but the idea seems to have eluded them. Even John had written in 2:22, likely in retrospect, "So when He was raised from the dead, His disciples remembered that He had said this." Soon their eyes would be opened and their memories refreshed by His actual appearances to them. In the meantime, they depart the garden for their homes to ponder the scene they had witnessed and consider their options.

Why did they not go forth and shout to the rooftops that Jesus was alive and then go forth to continue His ministry? Perhaps they needed to be further convinced that He, indeed, did come alive; perhaps they needed to integrate the facts that they had observed with the spirit which they felt; perhaps they just needed more time to collect their thoughts and prepare their message.

As disappointed as they were that Jesus did not emerge as a political figure or an earthly king, they would soon recognize that the prophecies of the Messianic age had been fulfilled. In the life, death and resurrection of Jesus, God had brought a climax to His dealings with His chosen people in history,[106] and the concluding act of this final "sign" has come to a close. The Messiah is now the Messiah for all people for all the ages to come.

The Appearance to Mary, 20:11-18

Distraught to be sure, Simon, the other disciples and the women, including Mary, have departed to their homes. Later, Mary alone returns to the tomb. Overwhelmed by grief, she weeps as she remembers her Master. Not as confident as the others, her chief concern is the grave robbery that she believes has occurred. Looking inside the sepulcher, she observes two angels, one at the head and one at the feet where Jesus would have lain. All four Gospels describe a form of angel at the tomb, yet Mary was not at all fearful or confounded by her sighting. Her response to their question, v. 13, is a logical, natural response to a logical, natural question. She remained troubled by the possible removal of Jesus' body by someone.

Even as she turned around and gazed into the eyes of Jesus, she was unaware of His identity. Jesus, appearing

106. C. H. Dodd, *The Apostolic Preaching*, 38f, 214f.

in His new, spiritual body[107] spoke her name in a voice that she instantly recognized. Then comes her confession, "Rabbouni." Apparently by reflex action, she reached for His garment, afraid that He might once again disappear.

Jesus' response reveals His unique perspective of existence. He now abides between the physical realm of the earthly present and the spiritual realm of the heavenly future. His body has yet to be glorified and bring to full completion His work on earth. Once glorified, He can return to the heavenly abode of His Father and live forever in His glorified body.

Jesus implores Mary to go and tell the disciples that He will soon ascend to the Father. She obeys her Master and does not simply tell them, but announces enthusiastically to them all that she had experienced.

The Appearances to the Disciples and His Glorified Body, 20:19-21:14

In the narrative of John the Gospeler, most scholars agree that the writer's intent is to suggest that the ascension of Jesus to the Father took place between 20:11-18 and 20:19f. Jesus would have now taken on His glorified body that would allow Him to appear to the disciples as He did here three times following the resurrection.

The First Appearance, 20:19-25

The setting of the first appearance is the evening of resurrection day. The disciples had discovered an empty tomb, unexplained and, at that moment, unexplainable. Their fear had reached a fever pitch; they felt like prey

---

107. Not yet His glorified body.

being hunted down to meet the same fate as their Master. They, along with other unidentified believers, sought refuge from the Jews in a secluded room. Could this room have been the same room in which they shared the Last Supper with the Master? Perhaps. After all, it would have been familiar to them.

The doors were closed so that they would hear anyone coming or going through the doors. Jesus suddenly appears, a sign of the nature of His resurrected body. Only a glorified body, one touched by the Father on high, could be so transformed as to appear mysteriously from nowhere. It was miraculous! Even though real, He is no longer limited to the ordinary and mundane state of a material existence.

His first words, "Peace to you" perhaps remind the disciples of His last words in 16:33 before the crucifixion. There He had said, "I have told you these things so that in Me you may have peace." Now, to restore a measure of confidence in them, He once again declares a "peace" that passes understanding. But did they really recognize Him? The marks on His hands and feet established grounds for great joy as they recognized the reality standing before them.

Once more, Jesus declares, "Peace to you." This utterance is to be the foundation of their ministry; it gives them a sense of boldness necessary for their future mission, and it prepares them to engage in the important work of establishing the church and seeing it through its earliest development.

By "breathing on them," Jesus, the Logos, filled them with the Holy Spirit, for it comprised the Johannine Pentecost. ἐμφυσάω (emphusaō), "breathed on" is the same verb used in Genesis 2:7 when God breathed into Adam the breath of life. The parallel is not lost on the disciples. As God had breathed life into Adam, so Jesus breathed the

Spirit into His disciples. It was a creative act not unlike the original creative act of the Logos in Adam.

The words of v. 23 have often presented a challenge. Does Jesus impart to the gathering in the room the power to forgive sin? No, indeed! The tenses of the verbs employed in this verse clarify the intended meaning. The disciples have been "sent," v. 21, on a mission to preach the completed mission of Christ to the world. By so doing, those who accept the death and resurrection message in faith have their sins forgiven. Both verbs, ἀφίημι (aphiēmi), forgive and κρατέω (krateō), retain, are written in the perfect tense. Best translated "have been forgiven" and "have been retained," these verbs point to an action that has been determined beforehand, not granted upon the acclamation of a disciple. As the church, we have the right to proclaim forgiveness of sins to those who willingly accept Christ, but we do not have the power or authority for such forgiveness. Thus the mission of the church clearly is to declare faith in Christ as the means of forgiveness of sins. Those who accept this faith have already been forgiven of sin.

The Appearance to Thomas, 20:24-29

At the time of the first appearance to the disciples, Thomas was not present. Eight days later, with Thomas counted among the disciples, Jesus appeared with them once more with the greeting stated previously in v. 19. Same room, same doors shut, same circumstances. Jesus appears miraculously.

Thomas can best be characterized as both a "courageous pessimist (11:16) and an honest skeptic (14:5)."[108] He was a man who, though faithful to his Lord, demanded a plausible explanation for what his mind could

108. Buttrick, *op. cit.*, 798.

not grasp. A living Jesus, even the Jesus that he had known and heard speak of resurrection, did not appear within the realm of logic to his rational mind. So, he demanded proof. And rightly so.

Even today, skeptics ask, "How do you know that Jesus rose from the dead?" Through the life and faith of Thomas, one can be assured that the Jesus who suffered, bled and died on Calvary's Cross, is the same Jesus who willingly exposed to Thomas the marks of His sacrifice. It proclaims the very purpose for which the Fourth Gospeler wrote his work. Unwilling to accept the experience and testimony of his best friends, Thomas sees for himself and confesses unashamedly his faith, "My Lord and my God!" With these words, Thomas banished all doubt and surrendered in faith and in loyalty to his risen Master. With these words, the truest confession of the Risen Saviour, the final "sign" is complete. With these words, John concludes his Gospel.

The Purpose of the Fourth Gospel, 20:30-31

Strachan describes this section of John's writing as a "postscript by the author."[109] Nowhere in all the Gospels is the dedicated intent so perfectly specified. Being familiar with the writings of Mark and Luke, John notes that the body of material on Jesus' life contains many more events upon which he could have drawn. But they did not fit his purpose. He, therefore, limits the events he cites to those that precisely suit his objective.

His aim, v. 31, is neither confusing nor indistinct. He wishes to illustrate, by his writings, the true nature of Jesus. Declaring through his work that Jesus was as much human as he was divine and as much divine as He was human, John unites these ideas in the person of one Man,

109. Strachan, *op. cit.*, 333.

Jesus Christ. He is not some theological pronouncement or founder of a humanistic idealism. Rather, He is the Christ, the revealed Son of God. Life, true life, comes only through believing in Him.

Commission of the Risen Christ to New Israel, 21:1-25

Chapter 21 of John's Gospel is considered almost unanimously as an epilogue, written after the original. On the one hand, Strachan maintains that "no convincing arguments have been brought forward, in my opinion, sufficient to discredit the hypothesis that this chapter is a very early addition to the Gospel, by an unknown author."[110] Canon B. H. Streeter, on the other hand, supports the thought that chapter 21 is an afterthought and, although it might have been authored by a "pupil of the author saturated in his master's spirit," it most likely stood as a part of the original Gospel.[111] Its style and character favor authorship by the original Gospeler. Whether a later addition or simply an afterthought of the Gospeler, it provides a fitting finale to the work of the Evangelist.

The Appearance of Jesus at the Sea of Tiberias, 21:1-14

The setting is the Sea of Tiberias, a reference only found in John. Simon Peter elects now to return to his former occupation and to cast out on the sea and fish. When he tells the other disciples about his decision, they ask to join him. So Simon, Thomas, Nathaneal, James and John, and two other unnamed disciples join Peter in the

---

110. *Ibid.*, 334.

111. B. H. Streeter, *The Four Gospels: A Study in Origins*, London: MacMillan and Company, LTD, 1930, 471-474. See also Plummer and Hoskyns.

boat. The two unnamed disciples might have been Andrew and Philip. Although the conclusion is speculative, one of the two unnamed disciples must be the author, John the Gospeler himself. The wording of this passage is of such detail that it could only have been written by someone who actually witnessed the event. Such a conclusion would be supported by v. 7, where John is referenced as the first to identify Jesus on the shore.

So out they go, fishing through the night with no success. "Caught" in v. 3 is unique to the Gospel of John. Πιάζω (*piazō*), meaning to take hold of or catch, occurs six times in John besides its later use in v. 10. Did it have meaning beyond the obvious? Perhaps. After all, the concept of fishers of men became common in the vocabulary of the early Christian church, especially based upon the reference in Mark 1:17.

Out of the haze of the morning, Jesus appears on the beach, unidentified by the disciples. His question to them (v. 5) commands a "no" answer as indicated by the emphatic Greek negative, οὐ (*ou*). Jesus knew the answer before He asked it. He wanted them to admit their lack of success.

"Cast the net on the right side of the boat," Jesus ordered. They obeyed the suggestion thinking that this "stranger" on the beach may have eyed a school of fish as a dark spot moving through the water on the right side. There is no hint here to suggest prescience or pre-knowledge on the part of Jesus.

The resulting draught of fish is most unusual. Attempting to drag the nets into the boat, John recognizes and acknowledges that the "stranger" on the beach is Jesus. He is the first to speak. But Peter, characteristic of his impulsive ways, upon hearing the words of John, is the first to act. He jumps into the water and swims the short distance to shore. Soon he is joined on the beach by the others in the boat.

Jesus had prepared a charcoal fire on the beach, and on that fire he had spread fish and bread for cooking. Yet, in spite of there being fish on the fire, Jesus asked Peter to bring fish from the net. Why would Jesus have made such a request of Peter when fish were already on the fire?

A bit of word study might help to understand the passage better. In v. 9 and v. 10 the noun describing the fish is ὀψάριον (*opsarion*), a word which typically refers to "whatever is eaten with bread, broiled or roasted."[112] The term employed in v. 11, however, is ἰχθύς (ichthus) which actually means "fish." It would later become the universal symbol of the Christian faith.

Due to constant persecution, early Christians developed a secret code for identity that included the symbol of the fish. Upon meeting another person on the street, a Christian might use his feet or finger to draw a small arc in the sand. If the other person were a Christian, he would draw another arc onto the one already drawn, completing the simplistic image of a fish.

How did the fish become the symbol of Christianity? The letters of the term ἰχθύς (*ichthus*), "fish," actually form an acrostic that describes Jesus. The first letter, ἰ, iota, is the first letter for Ἰησοῦς (*Iēsous*), the Greek name Jesus. The second letter, χ, chi, represents Χριστός (*christos*), the Greek word for "Christ." The third letter, θ, theta, denotes θεός (*theos*), "God." The fourth letter, ὑ, upsilon, designates υἱός (*huios*), translated "Son." And the fifth letter, ς, sigma, represents σωτήρ (*sōtēr*), "Saviour." Thus the symbol of the fish summarizes all that Jesus is and His purposeful mission on earth in one word, Jesus, Christ, God, Son, Saviour. Thus it became a symbol of the faith.

112. Thayer, *op. cit.*, 471.

Did the number of fish, specifically stated to be 153, have a meaning not readily evident? Perhaps so. The number 153 is considered to be the most complete of all numbers. Considering the importance of the number three, if the number one is cubed, the result is one; cubing the five results in 125; cube the three and the result is 27, totaling 153. By cubing these numbers, a sense of completeness might be inferred. These men had fished all night, and on their own, they had caught nothing. By following the command of Jesus, they realized success. So by including such a specific number, John may have been emphasizing the need for complete dependence upon Jesus. In obedience, one's life is complete.

Hoskyns traces the meaning of the number of fish through a diagram based upon Greek mathematics. Additionally, he states that "Greek zoologists held that there were 153 different kinds of fishes."[113] Perhaps this event could have been an extension of Jesus' parable in Matthew 13:47-48: "The kingdom of heaven is like a large net thrown into the sea. It collected every kind of fish, and when it was full, they dragged it to shore, sat down, and gathered the good fish into containers, but threw out the worthless ones." Interpretations vary as to the meaning of the fish including that they (1) represent the Christian church.[114] They are net gathering, and they are gathering the church together. Or, (2) they represent universal humanity as the ultimate goal of the church to reach.[115] If there is a hidden meaning to the Gospeler's intent in incorporating this number, it remains a secret only to him.

---

113. Hoskyns, *op. cit.*, 554. Jerome cited Oppian in his *Halieutica* that 153 species of fish were known at that time.

114. *Ibid.*

115. Strachan, *op. cit.*, 336.

The principal purpose of John for describing this occurrence is to record a third appearance of Jesus to the disciples following His resurrection. The number three was a vital symbol to John, and here it refers to completeness, fullness or totality. The mission of Jesus is complete because he has endured the Cross, was buried for three days, a period of time not lost on John, and He has been resurrected to a spiritual existence in which He will return to the Father and ultimately bring His children home with Him. His purpose is now complete, and John so declares it by emphasizing three post-resurrection appearances of Jesus.

The meal prepared by Jesus on the beach possesses Eucharistic overtones. John's words in v. 13, "took the bread, and gave it to them," are reminiscent of the words in Mark 14:22 at the Last Supper. While the quotation here is not intended to be Eucharistic in nature, it is naturally a reminder of that Supper which took place only a few days ago. Unknown as to how Jesus obtained the fish that had been placed on the fire prior to the disciples' arrival, the fish and the bread are truly a gift from the Risen Lord.

The Renewal of Peter, 21:15-17

Peter had often boasted with respect to his allegiance to Jesus. Nothing could deter Peter from following after his Master. In Luke 22:33, he declared his willingness to go to prison or even die for Jesus' sake. In Matthew 26:33, Peter expressed adamancy about his loyalty to Jesus. In Mark 14:31, Peter expressed a willingness to die with Jesus. So it was this Peter, the loyal, solid and often impetuous devotee to his Lord, now, after his denial, found himself in a somewhat uncertain position. Jesus will now force Peter to behold honestly and introspectively the true nature of his relationship with Him. The boasting has disappeared; the time for humility has come.

Notice that Jesus addresses him as "Simon Peter," consistent with the manner in which Jesus addressed him throughout the Gospel.[116] Jesus asks him three questions requiring three answers, all corresponding to the threefold denial by Peter in the courtyard. While no consensus exists with regard to the verb forms here, they do seem to possess significance as to the tenor of the encounter. Jesus asks the first question stating love as ἀγαπάω (agapaō), the highest and most expressive form of love.[117] Then Jesus adds the phrase "more than these." Somewhat ambiguous, could Jesus have been referring to Peter's greater love for Him than the other disciples, Peter's greater love for the other disciples over his love for fishing or perhaps his love for fishing and the nets over his dedication to Jesus and the mission to which he had been called? The context favors a reference, generally accepted, to his love for Jesus being more intense than the other disciples.

Jesus asks Peter a second time about love in its most forceful and personal form. Whether the idea simply escapes Peter's notice or whether he chooses to ignore the question in its purest form is unknown. His response, however, reveals much truth about Peter. He responds once more with φιλέω (phileō), a word describing warm affection or intimate friendship. Jesus must have been disappointed in Peter's response.

Peter had denied the Lord three times. Now he must avow his love for the Master for a third time. In the third questioning Jesus concedes the degree and character of Peter's

116. The only occurrence in the New Testament of Jesus addressing him as "Peter" is found in Luke 22:34.

117. Scholars like Strachan and Hoskyns consider the two words as interchangeable or even synonymous. Others such as Plummer, Abbott and Goodspeed take the position that the words are not interchangeable, and the Gospeler intended the conversation to juxtapose each question and response for heightened emphasis.

love and accedes to speaking the same word that Peter used in his answers, φιλέω (*phileō*). Notice that a third questioning by Jesus "grieved" Peter. For what reason might he be grieved? With all of the boasting of which he had been guilty, with all the impulsive acts he had committed as a disciple, with all his unquestioned devotion, he had not met the standard of love demanded of Jesus. And he finds it necessary to reiterate—yea, to emphasize—his love for Jesus in v. 17b. Yet, he continued to respond φιλέω (*phileō*). Nevertheless, Jesus accepts Peter's love at the point of his spiritual maturity.

After each response by Peter, Jesus commands him to feed the lambs or tend the sheep. His admonition is, in fact, a declaration of Peter's mission after Jesus ascends to the Father. Now the future assignment for which Peter had been prepared was about to begin. It is a mission requiring a humble spirit and a forthright determination to become God's spokesman on earth, His hands and His feet to a world crying out for a sense of purpose.

Jesus now knows that the restoration of Peter is complete. He has finished part one of the course. In spite of Peter's misgivings, Jesus, the second person of the Trinity who is all knowing, recognizes the steadfast love of Peter for his Lord, and He knows the Apostle's heart.

Peter's Death Foretold, 21:18-23

These words contain a prophecy of the manner in which Peter would give his life for the sake of Christ which occurred in Rome around AD 64. The girding by someone else refers to the routine the soldiers would use to strip him of his clothing. The stretching of his hands suggests that Peter was likely crucified which, tradition states, was head down.

The climax of Peter's restoration is in Jesus' words, "Follow Me." When spoken, Peter may have been reminded of his original call to discipleship by Jesus in Mark 1:17 where Jesus also promised to make him a fisher of men; perhaps he was taken back in his memory to the time when Jesus spoke of denying self and following Him. In this present context, "following" means more than accompanying Jesus as He proclaimed His message of salvation; now it would mean offering his own life, even unto death. The revival of Peter's commitment and perseverance is now complete. His ultimate restoration was described several centuries later by Isaac Watts.

> "But drops of grief can ne'er repay,
> The debt of love I owe—
> Here Lord, I give myself to thee
> 'Tis all that I can do."[118]

Final Words, 21:24-25

The final words of the Gospeler are yet another testimony corroborating 1:7 and confirm that what is written in this Gospel was witnessed by its author. Their character and tone comprise an appropriate climax of the Gospel, and any speculation of an author of 21:1-25 being anyone other than John himself seems to be laid to rest.

But to whom does the "we" of v. 24 refer? Plummer postulates that it may indicate the inclusion of other Apostles who join him in witness of the life of Christ and "guarantee the accuracy"[119] of the account. Plummer writes that "he adds their testimony to his own, and gives them a share in bearing witness to the truth of the Gospel."[120]

Whether others are included in this testimony or whether it is solely the witness of John, vv. 24-25 provide a

---

118. Isaac Watts, "At the Cross."
119. Plummer, *op. cit.*, 377.
120. *Ibid.*

coherent conclusion that follows naturally the flow of the entire narrative that goes before. John would later write another testimony in which he would proclaim, "What we have heard, what we have seen with our eyes, what we have observed and have touched with our hands, concerning the Word of Life" (1 John 1:1). The similarity of tones is unmistakable, confirming that John himself added this postscript later as a means of providing a fitting closing to his Gospel.

The words of v. 25 echo those of 20:30 and add an appropriate sense of dearth to the narrative. The Gospeler acknowledges that his intent was not to write an unabridged account of the life of Christ but to achieve a specific purpose, which he believes he has fulfilled. Origen so believed in John the Gospeler's authorship of this verse that he quoted it six times in his writings.

The concluding words of this verse are a reminder of their more modern counterpart.

> *"Could we with ink the ocean fill, And were the skies of parchment made;*
>
> *Were every stalk on earth a quill, And every man a scribe by trade;*
>
> *To write the love of God above Would drain the oceans dry;*
>
> *Nor could the scroll contain the whole, Though stretched from sky to sky."[121]*

---

121. From the song, "The Love of God" by Frederick M. Lehman. This final verse, originally attributed to Rabbi Johanan b. Zakkai in the first century AD, was found penciled on the walls of an asylum by a man reported to have been demented. These reflective words were discovered only after his death.

John attests to a fragmentary version of the life of Christ. But it is sufficient for us because it points us to Him who came from the portals of heaven in the form of a fleshly man, poured Himself out to a world, both Jew and Gentile, in a ministry of repentance and faith, and finally paid the ultimate sacrifice for our sins, the sins of those gone before us and the sins of those who shall come after us. Sufficient for all are the words of the Gospeler, "Here is the Lamb of God, who takes away the sin of the world!"

Conclusion

The Gospel of John is the Crown Jewel of the Scriptures. It is the simplest, and at the same time, the most profound book of the New Testament. We have seen how John blends history and interpretation, biography and theology in such a way as to allow the reader, seeing the Jesus of history, sees Him in the light of Christian experience. The Gospel is a witness to Truth and to the Divine Reality made known in Jesus Christ. It is truly the *summa Evangelii*.

BIBLIOGRAPHY

Abbott, Edwin A., *Johannine Vocabulary*, London: Adam and Charles Black, 1905.

Aldrin, Buzz, "Communion in Space," *Guideposts*, October 1970.

Apologia 3(2), 1994.

Arndt, William F. and Gingrich, F. Wilbur, *A Greek-English Lexicon of the New Testament*, Chicago: University of Illinois Press, 1957.

Buttrick, George Arthur, ed., *The Interpreter's Bible*, vol. viii, New York: Abingdon Press, 1952.

Dodd, C. H., *The Apostolic Preaching*

Drummond, James *An Inquiry into the Character and Authorship of the Fourth Gospel,* New York: Charles Scribner's Sons, 1904.

Eusebius, *History of the Church.*

Goodspeed, Edgar, *The Gospel of John*, Chicago: University of Chicago Press, 1917.

Hort, F. J. A., *The Way, The Truth, The Life*, London: MacMillan and Company, 1893, 124.

Hoskyns, Edwin Clement, *The Fourth Gospel*, London: Faber and Faber Limited, 1947.

Josephus, *Bellum Judaicum.*

Plummer, Alfred, *The Gospel According to John*, Cambridge: University Press, 1891.

Roberts, Alexander, *The Ante-Nicene Fathers*, The Christian Literature Publishing Company, 1885.

Robertson, A. T., *The Divinity of Christ in the Gospel of John*, New York: Fleming H. Revell Company, 1916.

Strachan, R. H., *The Fourth Gospel*, London: SCM Press, Ltd., 1941.

Strack, Hermann L. and Billerbeck, Paul, *Kommentar Neuen Testament aus Talmud und Midrash*, Munich: C. H. Beck'sche Verlagsbuchhandlung, 1922.

Streeter, B. H., T*he Four Gospels: A Study of Origins*, London: MacMillan and Company, LTD 1930, 471-474.

Tenney, Merrill C., "Topics from the Gospel of John, Part II: The Meaning of the Signs," *Bibliotheca Sacra* 132 (April 1975).

Thayer, Joseph Henry, *Greek-English Lexicon of the New Testament*, Grand Rapids: Zondervan Publishing House, 1962.

APPENDIX A

THE SIGNS OF JOHN'S GOSPEL

John writes in 20:30-31 that he authored his Gospel employing "sign" in order that "you may believe that Jesus is the Christ, the Son of God." While he did not write in mystical or mysterious terms, John did infuse certain events in the life of Jesus with more theological meaning and significance than did the Synoptists. They suited his purpose more effectively, and he could better connect them as fulfillment of prophecy.

While not all scholars view the "signs" in exactly the same way, I am taking the liberty to list those I believe complete John's purpose best. I have also offered a listing of the criteria described in chapter 2 to identify the "signs."

Sign 1: Changing Water into Wine at Marriage Feast (2:1-11)

Miracle: Jesus changes water into wine.

Participation: Servant who drew the wine.

Witnesses: Guests and headwaiter.

Messianic Significance: Jesus is the new wine drawn out of the old wine and who offers a superior new nature.

Sign 2: The Faith of a Gentile (4:43-54)

Miracle: Jesus healed the nobleman's son.

Participation: The faith of the nobleman.

Witnesses: The nobleman, his servants and his household.

Messianic Significance: Jesus is rejected by His own but accepted by a Gentile. Jesus is a universal Saviour for all mankind, Jew and Gentile alike.

Sign 3: Relation of Christ to the Sabbath (5:1-30)

Miracle: Jesus heals a man at the Pool of Bethesda on the Sabbath.

Participation: The healed man.

Witnesses: The healed man and others at the Pool of Bethesda.

Messianic Significance: Sabbath represents old Judaism. By healing on the Sabbath Day, Jesus declares the power of the Son through healing and the superiority of Christ over the oppressive Laws that governed the lives of the Jews of that day.

Sign 4: Christ as the New Manna from Heaven (6:1-14)

Miracle: Jesus feeds the 5,000.

Participation: The crowd fed by Jesus.

Witnesses: The crowd and His disciples.

Messianic Significance: The crowd represents the Old Covenant whose sustenance was the old manna provided in the wilderness. Jesus represents the new manna of a New Covenant.

Sign 5: Christ as the Light of the World (9:1-34)

Miracle: Jesus heals the blind man at the Pool of Siloam.

Participation: The blind man.

Witnesses: The blind man, others at the Pool, and Jewish leaders who questioned the man and ultimately excommunicated him.

Messianic Significance: The man is a type of the Old Covenant that is overshadowed by the Light of the New Covenant. Also, the event is a prophecy of Jesus' sacrifice in the spittle in which Jesus gives a part of Himself for the man's healing. Jesus opened the eyes of the blind man to the light, so He offered Light to His own people, even those who refused to accept the Light offered.

Sign 6: Christ as the Giver of New Life (11:1-46)

Miracle: Jesus raises Lazarus from the dead.

Participation: Lazarus.

Witnesses: Lazarus, his family and friends.

Messianic Significance: Lazarus is the type for the Old Covenant that is now dead in its efficacy to forgive sin. Jesus has come to raise out of that Old Covenant a new life.

Sign 7: Christ as the Source of Life (20:1-18)

Miracle: Jesus The Passion and Resurrection.

Participation: Jesus.

Witness: The disciples, Jesus' family, the Jewish ecclesiastics and the Roman authorities.

Messianic Significance: By His death and resurrection, Jesus completes His mission to offer to Old Israel and to the Gentile world a New Covenant based on love, paid for in blood and life-giving in its ultimate reality.

Appendix B

Numbers as Symbols in John's Gospel

John the Gospeler was a Jew who would have been quite familiar with the system of numerical meanings that came to be known as the Gematria. The Gematria is a system of numerical values attached to Hebrew letters that form the basis for certain ideas and concepts. By understanding the nature and meaning of these numerals, one can interpret the significance of words and phrases that appear in a particular biblical text.

Three – 3

Perfection, although to a somewhat lesser extent than seven. Perfection, in the case of this number, refers to spiritual perfection. Note its use in:

1. The three denials of Peters (18:17-27).

2. Jesus' death at 3:00 p. m. (19:30).

3. Jesus was buried three days before His resurrection (20:1-8).

4. Jesus' three questions to Peter regarding his love for the Lord (21:15-17).

5. Jesus' three appearances to the disciples following the resurrection (20:19-21:14).

Five – 5

God's grace, goodness and favor towards humans, redemption. The meaning of this numeral is best illustrated by the woman at the well (4:7-26). Having been married five times she most needed the grace, mercy and favor of Jesus at this moment, and in this moment, Jesus offered His grace and favor to her.

Another demonstration of the meaning of this number is found at the feeding of the five thousand (6:1-14). These were people in need of redemption, in need of the message of grace and salvation which Jesus was offering. The fact that there were five thousand of them highlights this very point. Add the fact that Jesus fed them from a lunch of five loaves, reinforces the message of this numeral even more.

Six – 6

Man, less than perfect, human weakness, sin. Note that the key use of this numeral is at the wedding in Cana where Jesus orders the drawing of water from the six water pots (2:1-11). These six water pots represent the imperfect Israel out of which the perfect Messiah would emerge.

Seven – 7

Spiritual and physical perfection and completion. John's highest motive in writing his Gospel was to "prove" that Jesus was the Christ. For this reason, he presented his Gospel in seven signs. By doing so, he emphasized the nature of this numeral. The fact that he portrayed seven signs is indicative of his desire to reveal that this Jesus, from Nazareth in Galilee, was, indeed the Messiah, the perfect messenger sent from God to offer salvation to an imperfect world.

In addition to this global intent, John also interspersed several events throughout his Gospel to illuminate further the significance of this number.

1. Seven times in John he employs the term ὥρα (*hōra*), "hour," to refer to the time of Jesus' glorification, better referred to as His crucifixion.

2. Seven times the word ὕδωρ (*hudōr*), "water," is used metaphorically in the Gospel, as seen most explicitly in 19:34.

3. John introduces the "I AM" sayings of Jesus. Seven times he writes , ἐγώ εἰμί (*egō eimi*), "I AM," to refer to the divinity of Christ.

4. In the passion narratives, John dramatically presents seven scenes during the Roman trial to represent the completeness of Jesus' sacrifice.

Ten – 10

Complete and perfect number. The most direct use of this number in John's Gospel is in the ten manifestations about which he wrote. These manifestations offer insight into the character of the Messiah and point to a spiritual meaning beyond themselves.

Twelve – 12

Also considered a perfect number in that it symbolizes God's power and authority. Additionally it points to a perfect governmental foundation. It can also symbolize completeness or the nation of Israel as a whole. The best illustration of this use of the numeral is at the feeding of the five thousand where twelve baskets of leftovers were gathered (6:1-14).

One danger for interpreters of the Bible is to read into the text more than is meant. This account of the use of numbers is included to enhance one's understanding of the importance and significance of such numbers in biblical writing. John employed these numbers for specific reasons because his intent in writing went beyond a simple and mundane explanation about the Messiah. He wished to apply cultural and religious symbolism in order that his readers might comprehend more fully that Jesus is the Christ for whom they have waited for so long.

Appendix C

The Seven "I Am" Sayings of Jesus from John's Gospel

Jesus said "I AM" on seven occasions. Each "I AM" is a description Jesus gave of Himself and is recorded in John's Gospel. All of these statements are characterized by their form in the original language. They are exclusively comprised of the words, ἐγώ εἰμί (*egō eimi*). The seven "I AM" sayings help us better understand the divinity of Jesus Christ.

1. Bread: "I am the bread of life; he who comes to Me will not hunger." *John 6:35*

2. Light: "I am the light of the world; he who follows Me will not walk in the darkness, but will have the light of life." *John 8:12*

3. Door: "I am the door; if anyone enters through Me, he will be saved, and will go in and out and find pasture." *John 10:9*

4. Good Shepherd: "I am the good shepherd; the good shepherd lays down His life for the sheep." *John 10:11*

5. Resurrection and Life: "I am the resurrection and the life; he who believes in Me will live even if he dies." *John 11:25*

6. Way, Truth, Life: "I am the way, and the truth, and the life; no one comes to the Father but through Me." *John 14:6*

7. True Vine: "I am the true vine, and My Father is the vinedresser." *John 15:1*